AF600331

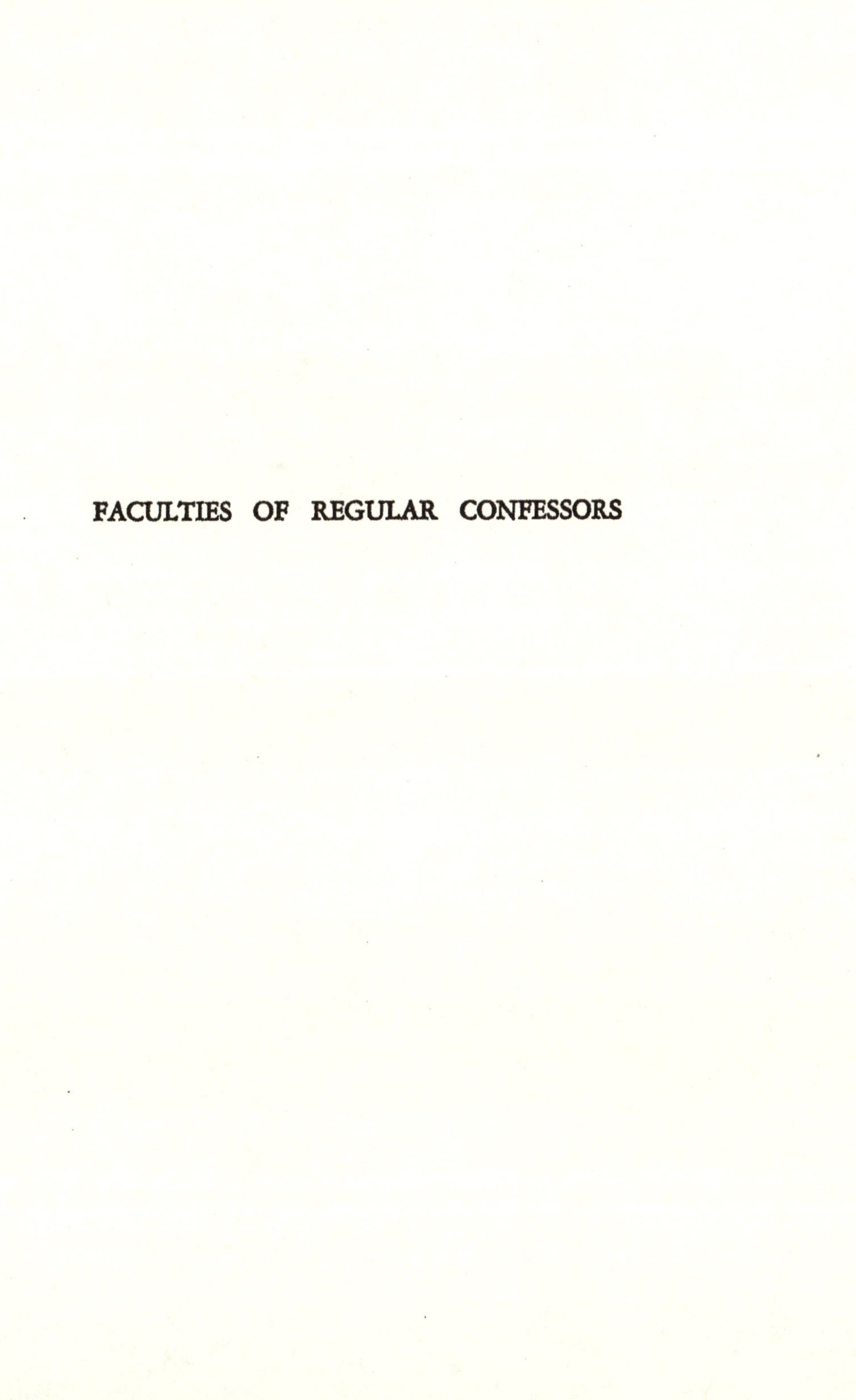

FACULTIES OF REGULAR CONFESSORS

THE CATHOLIC UNIVERSITY OF AMERICA
CANON LAW STUDIES
No. 280

Faculties of Regular Confessors

A HISTORICAL SYNOPSIS AND A COMMENTARY

BY THE

REVEREND MARCELLUS A. McCARTNEY, O.F.M., M.A., J.C.L.
PRIEST OF THE NEW YORK PROVINCE OF THE
MOST HOLY NAME OF JESUS

A DISSERTATION

SUBMITTED TO THE FACULTY OF THE SCHOOL OF CANON LAW OF
THE CATHOLIC UNIVERSITY OF AMERICA IN PARTIAL
FULFILLMENT OF THE REQUIREMENTS FOR THE
DEGREE OF DOCTOR OF CANON LAW

THE CATHOLIC UNIVERSITY OF AMERICA PRESS
WASHINGTON, D.C.
1949

Imprimi Potest :

BERTRANDUS J. CAMPBELL, O.F.M.

Minister Provincialis.

Neo-Eboraci, die 12 iulii 1948.

Nihil Obstat :

HIERONYMUS D. HANNAN, A.M., S.T.D., LL.B., J.C.D.

Censor Deputatus.

Washingtonii, D.C., die 3 iunii 1948.

Imprimatur :

✠ PATRITIUS A. O'BOYLE, D.D.

Archiepiscopus Washingtoniensis.

Washingtonii, D.C., die 3 iunii 1948.

THE ACADEMY PRESS
WASHINGTON 14, D.C.
Printed in U.S.A.

To the
Franciscan Order

TABLE OF CONTENTS

FOREWORD

The purpose of the coming of our Lord and Saviour, Jesus Christ, was to give to men the gift of divine life: He came that they might have life and have it more abundantly. In the fulfillment of the purpose of the coming of the God-made-Man the sacrament of penance plays a vital rôle, for it is through this wonderful sacrament that spiritual death gives place to life, and life possessed is rendered more fruitful.

Anything connected with this sacrament of mercy should be of tremendous interest to men. Hence the appearance of a dissertation such as this needs no excuse. However, for its particular appearance at this particular time a word of explanation must be given.

The present thesis is intended to supplement in some small way the fine study written five years ago by the Reverend Ralph Vincent Shuhler, O.S.A., J.C.D. In his work entitled *Privileges of Regulars to Absolve and Dispense,* Father Shuhler covered the wide field of the privileges of Regulars in relation to the absolution from those automatic censures which are reserved to the ordinary by the Code of Canon Law, to the dispensation and commutation of vows, and to the dispensation from irregularities.

In the present work the writer has omitted any detailed treatment of the dispensation from vows and irregularities, and has limited himself to a discussion of the sources and the extent of the confessional jurisdiction of the Regular confessor and to an explanation of the censures from which he can absolve in virtue of his privilege. Since the study follows and is based upon the dissertation written by Father Shuhler, the writer feels obliged to express his indebtedness and his gratitude to him.

It is difficult to acknowledge adequately the various influences that have entered into the formation of one's life and character. Of such influences, some are visible, others invisible; some are remembered, others forgotten. It is just as difficult to acknowledge the factors that have contributed to the fruits of one's labors. Many persons have undoubtedly entered, in one way or another, into the task of composing the present dissertation. The author wishes to thank each and every one of them, whoever they may be, He wishes to express his heartfelt gratitude in particular to his parents, to his teachers, to his superiors, to the Franciscan Province of which he is proud to be a member, and to the Faculty of the School of Canon Law at the Catholic University of America. All have played a part in the formation of the present work; all have had a share in bringing it to a successful conclusion.

PART I

HISTORICAL SYNOPSIS

INTRODUCTION

The present dissertation proposes to treat of the confessional jurisdiction and faculties of Regular priests alone, that is, of those religious priests who have professed the Rule of an approved Order, who are members of an institute of solemn vows.

Up until the sixteenth century practically all religious foundations embraced some one of the four great Rules as their mode of life: the Rule of St. Basil, of St. Benedict, of St. Augustine, or of St. Francis[1] In the sixteenth and seventeenth centuries other Orders arose which were not based on any of the foregoing Rules.[2]

As history testifies, the religious Orders played an important rôle in the active ministry. For the exercise of this ministry religious priests were invested with confessional jurisdiction.

The special confessional faculties enjoyed by the individual Orders were gradually extended to all the Orders by means of a canonical institution known as the intercommunication of privileges. By means of this institution the privileges of one Order became the common property of the others.[3] This institution has rightly been called *the privilege of acquiring privileges.*[4]

---

[1] Cf. Zeiger, *Historia Iuris Canonici* (2 vols., Romae: apud Aedes Universitatis Gregorianae, 1939 - 1940), I, nn. 111-119. The Carmelites, for example, constitute an exception to the general statement given in the text inasmuch as they profess a Rule not included in any of the four just mentioned.—Zeiger, *ibid.*, n. 118

[2] E.g., the Theatines and Jesuits. Cf. Zeiger, *ibid.*, nn. 112 and 120. For a treatment of the religious state and of the development of the religious Orders confer also Ramstein, *A Manual of Canon Law* (Hoboken, N.J.: Terminal Printing and Publishing Co., 1947), pp. 286 - 289 (hereafter cited *Manual*).

[3] Cf. Mocchegiana, *Iurisprudentia Ecclesiastica* (3 vols., Quaracchi, 1904 - 1905), I, n. 677.

[4] Mocchegiani, *ibid.*, n. 683.

The first instance of such intercommunication occured in the pontificate of Pius II (1458 - 1464).[5] On October 5, 1462, Pope Pius communicated or shared the privileges of the Cassinese Benedictines with the Benedictines of Mount Olivet.[6]

It was, however, Sixtus IV (1471 - 1484) who really introduced it on a large scale. He communicated the privileges of the Mendicant Orders with the Hermits of St. Augustine on February 7, 1474 [7] and with the Order of Minims of St. Francis of Paula on May 27, 1474 [8] On August 31, 1474, the same pontiff granted the mutual interchange of privileges between the Franciscans and the Dominicans. [9]

All of the foregoing were more or less particular grants. The first example of a general sharing of privileges with a larger group of Orders is contained in the Constitution *Dudum per nos*, issued by Leo X (1513 - 1521) on December 10, 1519. [10] In this constitution the supreme pontiff mentioned by name the six Mendicant Orders that were in existence in his day: the Order of Friars Preachers, the Order of Friars Minor, the Order of Hermits of St. Augustine, the Order of Carmel, the Order of the Servites of Mary, and the Order of Minims of St. Francis of Paula. Pope Leo decreed that these six Orders all shared in the privileges previously granted to any one of them, and that they possessed the perogative of participating likewise in the privileges that

[5] Capobianco, *Privilegia et Facultates Ordinis Fratrum Minorum* (Salerno: ex conventu S. M. Angelorum, 1946), n. 12 (hereafter cited *Privilegia*).

[6] Const. *Licet ex debito*, § 12—*Bullarum Diplomatum et Privilegiorum Sanctorum Romanorum Pontificum Taurinensis editio* (25 vols., Augustae Taurinorum, 1857 - 1872), V, 172 (hereafter cited *Bull. Rom. Taur.*).

[7] Const. *Dum fructucs uberes*—*Bullarium Ordinis Eremitarum S. Augustini* (ed. L. Empoli, Romae, 1628), 347. The reference and citation is given by Shuhler, *Privileges of Regulars to Absolve and Dispense*, The Catholic University of America Canon Law Studies, n. 186 (Washington, D.C.: The Catholic University of America Press, 1943), pp. 18-19 (hereafter cited *Privileges of Regulars*).

[8] Const. *Sedes Apostolica*, § 9—*Bull. Rom. Taur.*, V, 215.

[9] Const. *Regimini universalis ecclesiae*, § 16—*Bull. Rum. Taur.*, V, 221. Cf. Capobianco, *loc. cit.*

[10] *Bull. Rom. Taur.*, V, 732; Capobianco, *op. cit.*, n. 13.

might be granted to any one of them in the future by him and by his successors, just as though these privileges had been granted to each one directly.

The intercommunicative sharing of privileges was based on a twofold reason: first of all, on the equal esteem and benevolence which the popes had for the Mendicant Orders; and secondly, on the equal labors and merits of the Regulars in their apostolic work.[11]

After the Council of Trent (1545 - 1563), Pius V (1566 - 1572) confirmed all the privileges of religious that were not contrary to the legislation of that council. [12] He then extended the privileges of the Mendicants to a group of non - Mendicant Orders [13] and afterwards to the Society of Jesus. [14]

In virtue of this latter papal document the Mendicants, in simple consequence of the approved principle of reciprocal participation, immediately shared in the privileges enjoyed by the Jesuits. A problem, however, eventually arose concerning the extent of this participation by the Mendicant Orders in the privileges granted to the Jesuits.

Gregory XIII (1572 - 1585) forbade to the Mendicants a participation in certain privileges bestowed upon the Jesuits. [15] It seems, however, that later popes revoked, at least implicitly, this restriction placed on the mutual sharing in these privileges.

---

[11] Cf. A Vasto, *De Communicatione Privilegiorum praesertim inter Religiones* (Aquilae, 1936), n. 9 (hereafter cited *De Communicatione*); Capobianco, *Privilegia*, n. 12.

[12] Const. *Etsi mendicantium*, 16 maii 1567—*Bull. Rom. Taur.*, VII, 573.

[13] Const. *Ex supernae*, 16 aug. 1567—*Bull. Rom. Taur.*, VII, 584. Cf. Matulenas, *Communication—A Source of Privileges*, The Catholic University of America Canon Law Studies, n. 183 (Washington, D.C.: The Catholic University of America Press, 1943), pp. 111-112 (hereafter cited *Communication*).

[14] Const. *Dum indefessae*, 7 iul. 1571—*Bull. Rom. Taur.*, VII, 923; Shuhler, *Privileges of Regulars*, p. 73.

[15] Const. *Pium et utile*, 22 sept. 1582—*Bull. Rom. Taur.*, VIII, 397. Matulenas, *Communication*, p. 112; Reiffenstuel, *Ius Canonicum Universum* (5 vols. in 4, Monachii, 1702 - 1710), lib. V, tit. 33, n. 63.

In the year 1591, Gregory XIV (1590 - 1591) granted to the Crosier Fathers a sharing in the privileges of all the Orders. [16] In the same year he granted the same privilege to the Clerks Regular for the Care of the Sick, specifically mentioning their sharing in the privileges of the Society of Jesus. [17]

Now, even prior to the Council of Trent (1545 - 1563), Clement VII (1523 - 1534) had already granted the Friars Minor a participation in the privileges of all the Orders, Mendicant and non-Mendicant. [18] And Clement VIII (1592 - 1605), in the year 1597, confirmed this common sharing of privileges in favor of the Friars Minor. [19] Therefore, the Friars Minor—and through them the other Mendicants—seem to have obtained a full participation in all the privileges granted to the Jesuits, inasmuch as they participated in the privileges of the Crosier Fathers and the Clerks Regular for the Care of the Sick, who in turn had completely been granted a sharing in the privileges of the Jesuits even after the restriction enacted by Gregory XIII.

Moreover, Clement VIII was very explicit in confirming the privileges of the Franciscans, He used words to the effect that his confirmation availed regardless of any previous restrictive, invalidating, or derogatory clauses employed by popes or religious superiors. [20]

In view of these facts it seems safe to conclude that the restrictive statement employed by Gregory XIII was revoked by subsequent popes, and that to the Mendicants was restored the full participation in privileges with the Jesuits.

Of course, there is no unanimous agreement among the authors about the answer to this problem. Rodriguez (+1613),[21] Reiffenstuel

---

[16] Const. *Romanus Pontifex*, § 3, 12 iul. 1591—*Bull. Rom. Taur.*, IX, 444.

[17] Const. *Illuis qui*, § 26, 21 sept. 1591—*Bull. Rom. Taur.*, IX, 479.

[18] Const. *Dum fructus uberes*, 30 maii 1525—Capobianco, *Privilegia*. n. 15; Mocchegiani, *Iurisprudentia Ecclesiastica*, I, n. 685. The writer could not find this constitution in the *Bull. Rom. Taur.*

[19] Const. *Ratio pastoralis*. § 3, 20 dec. 1597—*Bull. Rom. Taur.*, X, 387; Mocchegiani, ibid., n. 686.

[20] Const. *Ratio pastoralis*, § 5—*loc. cit.*

[21] *Quaestiones Regulares et Canonicae* (3 vols. in 1, Lugduni, 1613), t. I, q. 55, art. 17.

(1642 - 1703),[22] Ferraris (+c. 1763) [23] and Capobianco [24] maintain that the restrictive clause of Gregory XIII was revoked, and that consequently the Mendicants share in all the privileges of the Jesuits. Suarez (1548 - 1617) [25] and Schmalzgrueber (1663 - 1735) [26] maintain the contrary. A Vasto in his argumentation upholds the latter, or negative, opinion. [27]

A few words must be said concerning the participation of all Regulars in the privileges of Regulars. Strictly regarded, the participation of each particular Order in the reciprocal exchange of privileges can be verified only by the existence of a papal constitution or instrument in virtue of which the Order has been granted this privilege.[28] However, before the promulgation of the Code of Canon Law it was the common opinion, according to Mocchegiana (1839-1905),[29] that this intercommunication existed among *all* religious Orders, both Mendicant and non-Mendicant.[30]

In the study of the faculties of Regular confessors, it is necessary to keep in mind the existence of this acknowledged intercommunication of privileges. All Regulars share in it.

---

[22] *Ius Canonicum Universum*, lib. V, tit. 33, n. 64.

[23] *Prompta Bibliotheca Canonica, Iuridica, Moralis, Theologica, necnon Ascetica, Polemica, Rubricistica, Historica* (8 vols., Romae, 1781 - 1784), "privilegium," art. 1, nn. 27-28 (hereafter cited *Bibliotheca*).

[24] *Privilegia*, n. 15.

[25] *Opera Omnia* (26 vols. in 30, Parisiis, 1856-1861), VI, lib. VIII, cap. 17, n. 8.

[26] *Ius Ecclesiasticum Universum* (5 vols. in 12, Romae, 1843 - 1845), lib. V, tit. 33, n. 89.

[27] *De Communicatione*, n. 87.

[28] Cf. Schmalzgrueber, *ibid.*, n. 87.

[29] *Iurisprudentia Ecclesiastica*, I, n. 681.

[30] This, of course, in no wise settles the controversy as to the *full* participation of the other religious Orders in the privileges granted to the Society of Jesus.

CHAPTER I

REGULARS AND CONFESSIONAL JURISDICTION

ARTICLE 1. REGULARS AND THE CONFESSIONS OF SECULARS

A. The Pre-Tridentine Era

The monastic foundation, laid by St. Paul the Thebite (228 - 341) and developed by both St. Anthony of Egypt (251 - 356) and St. Pachomius (c.292 - 346), reached its full stature in the East with the Rules of St. Basil the Great (c.329 - 379). These Rules became the "way of life" for practically all Oriental monks. [1] The West became acquainted with monasticism through its contact with St. Athanasius of Alexandria (c.295 - 373). The latter, coming to Rome in the year 340, brought with him a life of St. Anthony which he had written; this work wrought a tremendous influence in the beginnings of the monastic life in the West. [2]

Western monasticism had its most famous founder in St. Benedict of Nursia (c.480 - 547), who composed his Rule at Monte Cassino about the year 528. [3] True, St. Benedict was neither the first nor the

---

[1] Cf. Guggenberger, *A General History of the Christian Era* (3 vols.: Vol. I, 18. ed., 1931; Vol. II, 16. ed., 1931; Vol. III, 13. ed., 1928, St. Louis: Herder, 1928-1931), I, n. 205; Poulet, *A History of the Catholic Church* (translated from the fourth French edition by Rev. Sydney A. Raemers, 2 vols., St. Louis: Herder, 1935-1936), I, 190-191; Vascotti, *Institutiones Historiae Ecclesiasticae Novi Foederis* (6. ed. recognita a Mathia Hiptmair, 2 vols., Vindobonae, 1895), I, 148-149, 320-321.

[2] Vascotti, *ibid.*, p. 321.

[3] Vascotti, *ibid.*, pp. 322-323; Poulet, *ibid.*, p. 290; Guggenberger, *ibid.*, n. 206.

only builder of monastic life in Europe. [4] Nevertheless, the Rule of St. Benedict became, in the course of time, the standard legislation for monastic life in the West. [5]

The fifth century discloses the beginnings of ecclesiastical legislation with regard to the monastic institution in both the East and the West. Since the Eastern monks were frequently a cause of trouble, the Council of Chalcedon (451) found it necessary to put them under the supervision of the bishop. [6] Although the monks of the West were not so unruly, the occasion arose to make laws for them. In about the year 455 a council was held at Arles with a view to settling a dispute that had arisen between Faustus, abbot of the monastery of Lérins, and Theodore, bishop of Fréjus, in whose diocese Lérins was situated. The Council decided that the bishop had jurisdiction over all matters pertaining to the administration of the sacraments and to ecclesiastical government, while everything else was left subject to the rule of the abbot. [7] The regulations of the Council of Arles soon found widespread application in the Western Church. [8]

In great majority the monks in the early days of monasticism were laymen. Due to force of circumstances, however, more and more of them were ordained to the priesthood. During the pontificate of St. Gelasius I (492-496), for example, the ranks of the clergy in

[4] Western monasticism can number among its founders and foremost exponents men like St. Martin of Tours (c.316-c.397), St. Honoratus of Lerins (c.350-429), John Cassian (c.360-c.435), and St. Caesarius of Arles (470-543).—Cf. Zeiger, I, n. 113.

[5] Dawson, *The Making of Europe* (New York: Sheed and Ward, 1945), p. 205.

[6] Cf. canon 4—Schroeder, *Disciplinary Decrees of the General Councils*, Text, Translation, and Commentary (St. Louis: Herder, 1937), pp. 92, 519 (hereafter cited *General Councils*); Matulenas, *Communication*, p. 90.

[7] Duchesne, *Early History of the Christian Church* (translated from the fourth French edition by Claude Jenkins, 3 vols., London: Murray, 1931-1938), III, 25; Mansi *Sacrorum Conciliorum Nova et Amplissima Collectio* 25; Mansi, *Sacrorum Conciliorum Nova et Amplissima Collectio* (53 vols. in 60, Parisiis, 1901-1927), VII, 907.

[8] Duchesne, *ibid.*, p. 26.

Lucania, Brutium, and Sicily had been so decimated by the ravages of both war and plague that scarcely a priest could be found to minister to the needs of the people. Because of the necessity for priests the Supreme Pontiff, on March 11, 494, granted a dispensation whereby candidates could be recruited from among the monks or the laity, provided they were of an upright life and were free from the impediments which he listed. [9]

Although he had been found useful and even necessary, the monastic priest experienced opposition to his labors in the external ministry. Perhaps the monastic ideal and vocation, as expressed by St. Jerome (c.342 - 420), was used as a pretext to hinder the monk in his pastoral work. In one of his letters the saint had declared that the work of a monk was not to teach, but to bewail his sins or those of the world, and to look forward in fear and trembling to the coming of the Lord; [10] in another, he had written that to be a monk meant to be alone, and that such solitude was not to be found in the cities. [11] At any rate, whatever the pretext, the claim was advanced that ordained monks could not use their priestly powers as did other priests. When the question was put to the supreme authority in the Church, St. Gregory I (590 - 604) came to the aid of these religious priests by

---

[9] C. 1. D. LV.; *Casus;* Jaffé, *Regesta Pontificum Romanorum ab condita Ecclesia ad annum post Christum natum MCXCVIII* (editionem secundam correctam et auctam auspiciis Gulielmi Wattenbach curaverunt S. Loewenfeld, F. Kaltenbrunner, P. Ewald, 2 vols., Lipsiae, 1885-1888), n. 636 (hereafter cited JL, JK, JE); Thiel, *Epistolae Romanorum Pontificum genuinae et quae ad eos scriptae sunt a S. Hilaro* (461-468) *ad S. Hormisdam* (514-523) (Brunsbergae, 1868), p. 362.

[10] Cf. c. 4, C. XVI, q. 1. The writer could not find this letter (*Ad Riparium adversus Vigilantium*) in either Migne, *Patrologiae Cursus Completus, Series Latina,* or the *Corpus Scriptorum Ecclesiasticorum Latinorum.* In a footnote to the chapter of the *Decretum* here cited, Friedberg stated that this letter of St. Jerome was not to be found in the Migne edition.—Cf. *Corpus Iuris Canonici* (editio Lipsiensis secunda, post A. Richteri curas instruxit A. Friedberg, 2 vols., Lipsiae, 1879-1881), I, col. 762, nota 26.

[11] Epistula LVIII, *Ad Paulinum Presbyterum,* 5—*Corpus Scriptorum Ecclesiasticorum Latinorum* (Vindobonae, 1866—), LIV, 533; c. 5, C. XVI. q. 1.

decreeing that it was lawful for them to preach, to baptize, to give Communion, to impose penances, and to absolve from sins. [12]

Monastic priests, then, possessed jurisdiction to hear confessions and to absolve from sins. Their activity in the parochial ministry was not at all singular in view of the need for priests. In the early days of Christianity the local church revolved around its bishop; he was *the* pastor, performing the priestly ministry himself. With the growth of the Church and the corresponding increase of duties, the bishop found it necessary to delegate some of his powers to his priests; from him they received a delegated jurisdiction to administer the sacrament of penance. Monastic priests were for a time subject to the bishop, and those of them who heard confessions received their jurisdiction from him either at the time of ordination or at the time of performing their priestly functions as confessors. In either case, the jurisdiction was delegated, and the bishop was the source of their faculties.

As one of the various factors which had influence on the administration of the sacrament of penance in the Western Church, the peculiar discipline of the Insular Church must be taken into account. The Insular Church embraced the Catholic Celtic communities in the British Isles, in Brittany (western Gaul), and in Spain in the very early Middle Ages. The ecclesiastical discipline common to such groups was not in perfect accord with that of the rest of the Church, a fact doubtless due to the isolation enjoined upon them in virtue not only of their natural geographical location but also of the troublesome times consequent upon the breaking up of the Roman Empire. Isolated as it was, then, it was but natural that the Insular Church should adapt its discipline to the characteristic traits of its people. The Celts had their own peculiar political structure; they were grouped into clans, tribes, and provinces. And each clan was independent and had its own monastery. The Insular Church, therefore, developed into a monastic church, without any such thing as a diocesan organization. The diocese, consisting of the monastery and the people surrounding it, was ruled by an abbot, who was scarcely ever invested with the episcopal character; his community might even include bishops, and these were

[12] C. 24, C. CVI, q. 1; *Casus;* JE. n. 1951.

subject to him just as were the others.[13] It was the abbot of the monastery who appointed priests for the administration of the sacrament of penance.

From the sixth century onward, the particular customs and discipline of the Insular Church were introduced into Gaul, South-Central Europe, and Northern Italy by Irish and Scottish missionaries, who came to the continent primarily to labor among their fellow Celts.[14] Thus, St. Columbanus (543-615) left Ireland with twelve companions for the continent. After his arrival in Gaul he discovered that, whether because of war or of episcopal negligence, religion was practically extinct, and the sacrament of penance was almost entirely neglected. He then undertook the task of revivifying Catholic life. At Luxeuil, in the Frankish Kingdom, the saint built a monastery, and to it people flocked for the "remedy of penance."[15] St. Columbanus apparently regarded all who came to his monastery as being under his jurisdiction, and he did not hesitate to absolve them from their sins, a practice which evoked a storm of protest from the secular clergy.[16]

That monastic priests continued to hear the confessions of the faithful who approached them is evident from the legislation enacted by the VI Council of Paris which was celebrated in 829. The Council did not look with favor upon the practice of the clergy and laity who went to the monasteries for confession in order to avoid going to the bishops and parish priests. It was decided, therefore, that monastic priests should administer the sacrament only to the monks of their own monastery.[17] This in reality amounted to a local decree on the neces-

---

[13] Zeiger, *Historia Iuris Canonici,* I. *De Historia Fontium.* p. 46. n. 40; idem, *op. cit.,* II. *De Historia Institutorum Canonicorum.* pp. 86-89. nn. 56-57.

[14] Zeiger, *Historia Iuris Canonici,* II. *De Historia Institutorum Canonicorum.* p. 89. n. 58.

[15] *Vitae Columbanae Abbatis Discipulorumque eius Liber* I, cc. 4, 5, 10—*Monumenta Germaniae Historica. Scriptorum Rerum Merovingicarum* Tomus IV. *Passiones Vitaeque Sanctorum Aevi Merovingici* (edidit Bruno Krusch, Hannoverae et Lipsiae, 1902). pp. 71, 72, 76.

[16] Cf. Shuhler, *Privileges of Regulars,* p. 7.

[17] C. 46—*Monumenta Germaniae Historica,* Legum Sectio III, *Concilia.* Tomus II. Pars II (recensuit Albertus Werminghoff, Hannoverae et Lipsiae,

sity of confessing to one's proper pastor, local legislation that was to be made universal almost four centuries later by the IV Lateran Council in 1215. [18]

In the course of time, an additional source of jurisdiction was bestowed upon the monasteries—papal jurisdiction. This was the result of the canonical institution known as exemption.

As applied to Regulars, exemption signifies their removal from the jurisdiction of the bishop, or from one who has ordinary authority in an ecclesiastical territory, and their immediate subjection to the Roman Pontiff, who governs them through their superiors. Such superiors exercise quasi-episcopal power with reference to their own subjects. [19]

The exemption of Regulars arose gradually, and various periods may be noted in its development. [20] Before the ninth century monastic exemption was bestowed only upon individual and outstanding monasteries. The first instance of complete papal exemption occurred in 628. On June 11th of that year, Honorius I (625 - 638), in answer to the petition of Bertulph (+640), abbot of the monastery of Sts. Peter and Paul at Bobbio, exempted that monastery from any and every jurisdiction other than that of the Holy See. [21]

From the ninth to the thirteenth century the privilege was granted

---

1908), p. 640; Thomassinus, *Vetus et Nova Ecclesiae Disciplina circa Beneficia et Beneficiarios* (10 vols., Moguntiae, 1787), pars I, lib. II, cap. 12, nn. 3, 4 (hereafter cited *Ecclesiae Disciplina*).

[18] C. 12, X, *de poenitentiis et remissionibus,* V, 38.

[19] Cf. Melo, *De Exemptione Regularium.* The Catholic University of America Canon Law Studies, n. 12 (Washington, D. C.: The Catholic University of America, 1921), p. 1; O'Brien, *The Exemption of Religious in Church Law* (Milwaukee: Bruce, 1943), p. 3; Bachofen, *Compendium Iuris Regularium* (New York: Benziger, 1903), p. 220.

[20] Cf. Bachofen, *op. cit.*, pp. 222-223

[21] *Bull. Rum. Taur.*, I, 178; JE, n. 2017; Kehr, *Regista Pontificum Romanorum, Italia Pontificia* (8 vols. in 10, Berolini, 1906-1935), VI, ii, p. 249, n. 6; Montalembert, *The Monks of the West* (2 vols., Boston, ?), I, 583: Shuhler, *Privileges of Regulars,* p. 5.

more extensively. It was in this period that the monastic congregations, or unions of the various isolated monasteries, appeared. And it was to the monasteries of these groups that the privilege of exemption was granted, while the individual monasteries that remained outside of the confederations were as a rule still subject to the bishop. At the dawn of the thirteenth century there were two classes of monasteries: the exempt and the non-exempt.[22]

In virtue of the privilege of exemption, the monasteries and the monastic subjects were withdrawn from the jurisdiction of the local ordinary. The latter could not bestow the necessary jurisdiction upon monastic priests for the confessions of the subjects of the monastery, since these were no longer subject to his authority. The source of the jurisdiction for the administration of the sacrament of penance to the members of the exempt monastery was the Roman Pontiff.[23] In some instances there was given to the exempt monastery a papal jurisdiction which permitted its priests to hear the confessions of any penitents who came to it, and to absolve them from their sins. On May 10, 1063, Alexander II (1061 - 1073) granted such a privilege to the monastery of Cluny.[24]

At the beginning of the thirteenth century the norm of jurisdiction of Regular confessors may be stated to have been as follows: their jurisdiction for the confessions of the subjects of their monastery came from the pope; their jurisdiction for the confessions of penitents who were not members of the monastery was conferred in certain cases by the pope, otherwise by the bishop. With the coming of the Mendicant Orders a radical change was soon introduced because of the fact that the priests of these Orders began to receive all their confessional jurisdiction and faculties from the Holy See.

---

[22] Reilly, *The Visitation of Religious*, The Catholic University of America Canon Law Studies, n. 112 (Washington, D.C.: The Catholic University of America, 1938), p. 45; cf. Reilly, *ibid.*, pp. 41-45.

[23] Cf. Wernz-Vidal, *Ius Canonicum* (7 vols. in 8, Vol. II 3. ed., 1943; Romae: apud Aedes Universitatis Gregorianae, 1925-1943), IV, i, 152, nota 15; Shuhler, *Privileges of Regulars*, p. 5.

[24] *Bull. Rom. Taur.*, II, 27-28; JL, n. 4513.

The Mendicant Orders were destined to play an important rôle in effecting the reform of the Church. The Holy See recognized this fact and gave the new movement its blessing. In one sense this movement cannot be called new, for it was rather the revivification of a power that had begun to lie dormant in the bosom of the Church: a life lived in accordance with the *entire* Gospel. In another sense, however, it was something new, for the Mendicants brought with them a new concept of the religious life.

The monasteries of the older Orders were independent of one another.[25] This was true even of those monasteries that were grouped into a congregation; in the monastic congregation the various houses were held together merely by a loose bond, each existing as a complete unit in itself. The autonomy of the individual community was brought into bold relief against the background of its location. The monks had built their monasteries in the solitude of valleys and country districts, and from the products of their land they derived sufficient income to provide for their livelihood. Their scheme of life was characterized by a note of stability; and, as a general rule, this stability was evident in their work in the apostolate in this sense, that the monks remained in their monasteries and the people came to them.

The Mendicants, on the other hand, formed a compact and closely-knit organization. Their convents were an integral part of the province, their provinces integral parts of the Order. There was one centralized authority, to which the entire organization was subject and under which it was united; this fact gave to the Mendicants a greater facility in carrying out the purpose of their life. The friars fixed their abodes in busy cities that were already throbbing with a new industrial life, and they depended for their livelihood on the benevolence of the people. And, finally, joining the active with the contemplative life, they left their dwelling-places, traversed the high-ways and byways in search of souls, and spiritually nourished these souls wherever they found them.[26] And in this questing for souls the sacrament of penance played a vital rôle.

---

[25] The *cellae* or daghter-houses founded by a monastery were still subject to the jurisdiction of the mother-house.

[26] Zeiger, *Historia Iuris Canonici*, II, *De Historia Institutorum Canonicorum*, p. 101, n. 68, 4b.

The Mendicants, however, would have been seriously handicapped in their apostolate had not the Holy See intervened to obviate a difficulty. Heretofore the pastoral care of souls had been subject to a regulation known as the "parochial bann." In other words, the faithful belonged to definite parishes and were subject to specified clerics in such a way that they could not go elsewhere for the reception of the principal sacraments. The Holy See, by means of privileges, rendered the "parochial bann" inoperative as far as the Mendicants were concerned. [27]

In the beginning of their history the Mendicants were not the recipients of these extraordinary favors simply for the reason that the Apostolic See held them in special esteem and wished to reward them. On the contrary, it seems that the Roman Pontiffs favored them and their cause as far as possible for the reason that they saw in these new organizations a tremendous factor to be utilized in the reformation of the clergy and the people. The question of reform was a burning issue at the time the Mendicant friars came into existence, and in them the popes must have believed they had found a solution.

At any rate, Cardinal Hugolin (c.1145 - 1241), the friend and admirer of Sts. Francis (1181 - 1226), and Dominic (1170 - 1221), did not forget the service that their friars were capable of rendering to the Church. In the year 1227 he ascended the throne of Peter under the name of Gregory IX (1227 - 1241), and in this the very first year of his pontificate he gave the first broad grant of faculties to a Mendicant Order, the Dominicans. In commending the Dominican priests to the prelates of the Church, the supreme pontiff stated that these friars had apostolic jurisdiction to hear confessions. [28]

The Mendicant Orders soon experienced opposition to their labors. An attempt was made to brand their ministry as illegal, but to no avail. In the year 1257, Alexander IV (1254 - 1261) championed the cause

---

[27] Zeiger, *ibid.*, pp. 101-102, n. 68, 4c.

[28] Const. *Quoniam,* 10 maii 1227: "... cum ipsis auctoritate nostra liceat cofessiones audire, ac poenitentias iniungere...."—Confettius, *Collectio privilegiorum sacrorum Ordinum Fratrum Mendicantium et non Mendicantium* (Florentiae, 1598), pp. 5-6 (hereafter cited Confettius).

of the friars and made it clear that they could preach and hear confessions with the permission of the Holy See, its legates, or the local ordinary, without any necessity of obtaining permission from inferior prelates or even parish priests.[29] This grant was practically repeated in the year 1265 by Clement IV (1265 - 1268); the latter pontiff, however, specifically excepted from the Mendicants' confessional faculties the sins which were reserved to the Holy See, to its legates, or to the bishops.[30]

Less than twenty years later the confessional jurisdiction of the Mendicants became territorially co-extensive with that of the pope. On December 13, 1281, Martin IV (1281 - 1285) empowered the Franciscan Minister General and Provincials, with their definitorium, to commit to the friars approved by them the offices of preaching, of hearing confessions, and of imparting absolution; the only condition he placed was this, namely, that those who confessed to the friars were bound to confess at least once a year to their parish priests in accordance with the law of the IV Lateran Council (1215),[31] and that the friars had to urge their penitents to do so.[32] The friars, in virtue of this papal constitution, were thus enabled to preach and to hear confessions anywhere and everywhere without the permission of either parish priest or bishop. The competency of the friars for the ministry was to be determined by their superiors.[33]

---

[29] Const. *Non sine multa,* 30 mart. 1257—*Bullarium Franciscanum* (editum studio et labore Joannis Hyacinthi Sbaraleae, tomi I-IV, Romae, 1759-1768), II, 209-210 (hereafter cited *Bull. Francisc.*); Gratien, "Ordres mendiants et clergé séculier a la fin du XIIIe siécle,"—*Etudes franciscaines,* XXXVI (1924), 499-501 (hereafter cited Gratien).

[30] Const. *Quidam temere,* 20 iun. 1265—*Bull. Francisc.,* III, 14.

[31] Cf. c. 12, X, *de poenitentiis et remissionibus,* V, 38.

[32] Const.*Ad fructus uberes*—*Bull. Francisc.,* III, 480. The same privilege was given to the Dominicans on January 10, 1282.

[33] Gratien, pp. 501-502. Shuhler (*Privileges of Regulars,* p. 14) seems incorrect in stating that the favor contained in the Constitution *Inter cunctas* of Benedict XI (1304) is "the only instance in the history of papal confessional privlieges in which some form of presentation of religious priests to the local Ordinary was not necessary." As will soon be evident, the constitution of Benedict XI contained in reality a representation of the legislation enacted by Martin IV in his Constitution *Ad fructus uberes.*

Such a sweeping grant of jurisdiction raised a storm of opposition among the secular clergy. To nullify the effect of the privilege the bishops in France determined to interpret the phrase of Martin IV relative to the canon of the IV Lateran Council as meaning that the faithful had to confess *all* their sins at least once a year to their proper pastor, regardless of the fact that they might have previously confessed some of these sins to another priest during the course of the year. In the year 1286 the representatives of the French episcopate presented their case at the court of Martin's successor, Honorius IV (1285-1287), in an effort to obtain papal confirmation of such an interpretation, together with a declaration that the friars could not absolve from cases reserved to the bishops. Honorius, however, died without making any official pronouncement, and the controversy dragged on.[34]

Benedict Gaetani was one of the cardinals present at the court of Honorius IV when the confessional privileges of the friars were attacked by the representatives of the French episcopate. Cardinal Gaetani defended the friars.[35] In the year 1290, while on a papal mission to Paris during the pontificate of Nicholas IV (1288 - 1292), he presided over a council held at the Church of St. Genevieve, and again he defended the friars against the grievances and complaints of the French clergy; by the papal authority given to him, he confirmed the Mendicant privileges granted in the constitution of Martin IV.[36]

Cardinal Gaetani was elected pope in the year 1294 and began to rule the Church under the name of Boniface VIII (1294 - 1303). Since the privileges granted by the Martinian Constitution *Ad fructus uberes* were still a source of trouble even in his pontificate, the Supreme Pontiff deemed it wise to make an attempt to determine the rights of both parties equitably. Like a "loving father who is pained at the inconveniences suffered by his children," Boniface VIII, in an effort

---

[34] Gratien, pp. 502-512.

[35] Idem, pp. 505-506.

[36] Callebaut, "Les Provinciaux de la Province de France au XIIIe siécle Notes, documents et études."—*Archivum Franciscanum Historicum,* X (1917). 347-349: Gratien, pp. 509-510.

to bring about peace and harmony, promulgated a new constitution, *Super cathedram,* on February 18, 1300.[37]

The new legislation enacted by Boniface VIII established a set and definite procedure by which the Dominicans and Franciscans had to abide if they wished to administer the sacrament of penance to the faithful. First of all, the superiors of these Mendicants had to present themselves either personally or by proxy before the local ordinary and ask permission for their friars to hear confession in his particular territory. Then they were to choose suitable and competent friars and present them to the bishop for permission to absolve the penitents who came to them. If the ordinary rejected any of those presented, others were to be substituted for them; if these were likewise rejected, the friars could go ahead and validly and licitly hear confessions and grant absolution.

The particular Mendicant confessor was to exercise these faculties only in the city or diocese for which his superior had appointed him. It seems that no special power over reserved cases was granted to the confessor, inasmuch as the pope explicitly stated that by this concession he did not intend to grant greater power than the law granted to parochial priests; the power to absolve from sins reserved to the bishop would have to be granted by the bishop himself.

The peace and harmony intended by Boniface VIII did not result. Noting this fact, Benedict XI (1303 - 1304), a former Master General of the Dominicans, repealed the work of his predecessor. The failure of his predecessor's efforts to produce concord was due, in the opinion of Benedict XI, to the abrogation, without any evident advantage or reason, of privileges enjoyed over such a long period of time.

Benedict then went on to state, in his Constitution *Inter cunctas,* promulgated on February 17, 1304,[38] that the friars chosen by their superiors to hear confessions could, with apostolic authority and without

---

[37] C. 2, *de supltuiris,* III, 6, in Extravag. com.; inserted by Clement V (1305-1314) in the decree *Dudum* (c. 2, *de sepulturis,* III, 7, in Clem.) of the Council of Vienne (1311-1312); *Bull. Francisc.,* IV, 498-500.

[38] *Bull Francisc.,* V, 11-14; c. 1, *de privilegiis,* V, 7, in Extravag. com.

the permission of any prelates, absolve the penitents who came to them.[39] He commanded the major superiors of the Franciscans and of the Dominicans to inform the bishops, out of a spirit of reverence for them, that they had chosen confessors, and to seek permission for their sacramental ministry. This permission, however, was not a necessary condition, for if the bishops refused to give it or neglected to reply, the friars were at liberty to hear confessions and to absolve their penitents.

Certain restrictions, however, were placed on the faculties of these Mendicant confessors. They could not, for example, absolve religious who were bound by their statutes to confess to their superiors, or who were forbidden by their superiors to confess to others. They could not absolve from sins or censures reserved to the bishops or to the Holy See, except in favor of penitents who were in danger of death; even in this latter case the penitent had to swear that if he recovered he would appear before the proper authority to receive the latter's mandate. And, lastly, the friars had to remind the people of their obligation to confess their sins to their proper pastor at least once a year.

Like Boniface VIII, Benedict XI had directed his efforts to the settlement of disputes and to the establishment of peace between the secular clergy and the Mendicants. Like Boniface VIII, Benedict XI failed. Another pope tried to settle the controversy. The complaints against the Mendicants were laid before the Council of Vienne (1311-1312), which had been convoked by Clement V (1305-1314). At this Council, on May 9, 1312, Clement V promulgated the Constitution *Dudum,*[40] in which he revoked the legislation of Benedict XI's Constitution *Inter cunctas,* and restored that of the Constitution *Super cathedram* of Boniface VIII.

Before a decade had passed, though, the arguments against the Mendicants again came to the fore. Jean de Pouilly (died after 1321), Doctor of Sacred Theology at the University of Paris, taught in his

[39] Note that this is practically a restoration of the privilege granted by Martin IV in his Constitution *Ad fructus uberes,* promulgated on December 13, 1281. Cf. *supra,* p. 18, note 33.

[40] *Bull. Francisc.,* V, 87, n. 196[a]; c. 2, *de sepulturis,* III, 7, in Clem.

sermons and lectures that those who confessed to friars invested with a general permission to hear confessions were bound to confess these sins again to their proper pastor; basing his views on the decree of the IV Lateran Council (1215) on annual confession,[41] he went so far as to say that neither the pope nor God could grant to anyone the general power of hearing confessions in such a way that the penitent would not still be bound to repeat these same sins in the annual confession to his parish priest.

On July 21, 1321, John XXII (1316-1334) condemned these views as false, erroneous, and contrary to Catholic teaching; the pope asserted that those who confessed to the friars were no more bound to repeat the confession than if they had, in accordance with the decree of the IV Lateran Council, confessed these sins to their parish priest.[42]

The legislation of Boniface VIII, Benedict XI, and Clement V concerning the confessional privileges of the Mendicants had, in the end, failed to restore peace and unity between the Regulars and the secular clergy; the flames of the controversy over the rights of each had never completely died out. At the V Lateran Council (1512-1517) the bishops petitioned Leo X (1513-1521) to revoke all the privileges of the Mendicants and to subject them to the common law. The rights of the Mendicants were defended by Thomas de Vio (1469-1534), more commonly known as Cajetan, Master General of the Dominicans (1508-1517), and Giles Antonini (1465-1532), more commonly known as Aegidius of Viterbo, General of the Hermits of St. Augustine (1506-1518).[43]

Leo X sought to settle the controversy, and to this end he pro-

[41] Cf. c. 12, X, *de poenitentiis et remissionibus*, V, 38.

[42] Const. *Vas electionis*—*c.* 2, haereticis, V, 3, in Extravag. com. Cf. Denzinger-Bannwart-Umberg, *Enchiridion Symbolorum, Definitionum et Declarationum de Rebus Fidei et Morum* (21.-23. ed., Friburgi Brisgoviae: Herder, 1937), nn. 491-493 (hereafter cited DB).

[43] Thomassinus, *Ecclesiae Disciplina*, pars I, lib. III, cap. 39, n. 5; Matulenas, *Communication*, p. 106; A Vasto, *De Communicatione*, nn. 21-22.

mulgated the Constitution *Dum intra* on December 19, 1516.[44] In virtue of this legislation the superiors of the Mendicants, if they had appointed friars to hear the confessions of seculars, were bound to present these friars to the bishop, if he requested it, or to his vicar. The bishop had the right to examine these priests on their knowledge of the sacrament of penance. If they were admitted by the bishop—*or if they were unjustly rejected by him*—penitents could satisfy their obligation of annual confession by confessing to them. The Mendicant friars, however, could not absolve from penalties inflicted *ab homine.*

B. The Tridentine Era

Trent, a little city in southern Tyrol, Austria, was the scene of one of the greatest events in the history of the Church. It was there that the plans for the real reformation of the Church were formulated and put into action. Convoked in the year 1545 by Paul III (1534-1549), the Council of Trent reached its last session only eighteen years later. It was in the year 1563 that the Council came to a close, and then had its degrees and definitions ratified by Pius IV (1559-1565).

Among the questions of disciplinary reform that confronted the Council, it seems but natural that it should consider a subject that had been a burning issue in the days of Boniface VIII (1294-1303), Clement V (1305-1314), and the Fathers of the V Lateran Council (1512 - 1517)—namely, the faculties and privileges of Regulars in relation to the sacrament of penance.

The Tridentine Fathers did consider this question, and they enacted legislation concerning it that remained fundamental up to the time when the present Code of Canon Law was promulgated. They decreed

---

[44] *Codics Iuris Canonici Fontes* (cura Emi Petri Card. Gasparri editi, 9 vols., Romae [postea Civitate Vaticana]: Typis Polyglottis Vaticanis, 1923-1939; Vols. VII-IX, ed. cura et studio Emi Iustininani Card. Serédi), n. 72 (hereafter cited *Fontes*).

that henceforth no priest, be he secular or regular, could validly hear the confessions of secular penitents, whether clerical or lay, unless he had a parochial benefice or was approved by the bishop.[45]

In the Constitution *Super cathedram* of Boniface VIII, episcopal permission was required in order that religious priests might hear the confessions of seculars; if, however, such permission was twice denied, Regulars could validly and licitly absolve their penitents. Even the Constitution *Dum intra* of Leo X, while demanding personal presentation of the Mendicant confessors if the ordinary requested it, nevertheless decreed that the friars could hear confessions if permission was unjustly denied. The Tridentine decree, on the contrary, demanded episcopal approbation for the confessor to the extent that without it, whether it was justly or unjustly denied,[46] Regulars could not absolve even validly.

The Council of Trent here spoke of "approbation" and not of "jurisdiction." Both of them were necessary, but they were not synonymous terms. By approbation the priest was judged competent for the duty of hearing confessions; by the grant of jurisdiction he was actually given the power to hear the confessions of definite subjects.[47] In the case of Regulars the bishop gave them approbation, but their jurisdiction came from the Holy See; the approval of the bishop enabled them to exercise their jurisdiction.[48]

---

[45] Sess. XXIII, *de ref.*, c. 15: "Although priests receive by ordination the power of absolving from sins, nevertheless the holy council decrees that no one, even though a regular, can hear the confessions of seculars, even priests, and that he is not to be regarded as qualified thereto, unless he either holds a parochial benefice or is by the bishops, after an examination, if they should deem it necessary, or in some other manner, judged competent and has obtained their approval, which shall be given gratuitously; any privileges and custom whatsoever, even immemorial, notwithstanding."—Schroeder, *Canons and Decrees of the Council of Trent* (St. Louis: Herder, 1941). pp. 173, 444.

[46] Cf. proposition n. 13 condemned by Alexander VII through a decree of the Holy Office on September 24, 1665—*Fontes*, n. 734; DB, n. 1113.

[47] Cf. Ferraris, *Bibliotheca*, "approbatio," art. 1. nn. 1-4.

[48] Cf. Ferraris, *ibid.*, n. 42. Rodriguez, *Quaestiones Regulares et Canonicae*, t. I, q. 59, art. 3, contains the following sample of a formula that could be used in seeking the approbation of the bishop: "Reverenndissime domine, dom-

Even a cursory glance at the papal documents promulgated during the years that followed the Council of Trent gives evidence of the fact that prior to the present Code of Canon Law episcopal approbation was the basis for the exercise of jurisdiction in the act of hearing the confessions of seculars.[49] It is true that St. Pius V (1566 - 1572) had decreed that the Tridentine legislation did not include the priests of the Mendicant Orders who were approved by their Generals or Ministers Provincial for hearing the confessions of both sexes of the faithful.[50] But, as a result of abuses on the part of the Mendicants, the same pontiff at a later date stated that all Regulars, even Mendicants, had to observe the decree of the Council of Trent.[51]

Gregory XV (1621 - 1623), in the Constitution *Inscrutabili,*[52] repeated verbatim the Tridentine decree regarding the necessity of either

---

inationi vestrae supplex orator frater N. salutem in Domino Iesu ac debitam cum pari animi submissione reverentiam. Cum iuxta privilegia praefato ordini nostro pridem a sanctissima Sede Apostolica concessa et intra corpus iuris inclusa confessarii eiusdem ordinis ad audiendas confessiones sacramentales saecularium poenitentium alicuius civitatis, vel dioecesis instituendi debeant praesentari Praelatis eorum, ut ab ipsis si eis videbitur examinentur, et approbationem obtineant, iuxta in ipsis privilegiis contenta, et a Concilio Tridentino approbata, ut bona ipsorum venia, gratia et licentia id faciant. Ideo quam humilissimo animo possum supplex ipse sublimem, atque amplissimam dominationem vestram etiam, atque etiam rogo et oro, idque bona, atque certa spe, quam vestra istius animi benignitas largissimam promittit, ut infrascriptos fratres legitime secundum nostri ordinis statuta ad idoneos pro vestra in ordinem nostrum benevolentia, et pro nostra in vestram benignitatem amplissimam devotione, habeat pro legitime praesentatis ac perinde admittat eos ad confessiones subditorum suorum audiendas, ac si omnia, quae iura pontificia in id requirunt omnino servata essent. Quo nos quoque speciali devotione, ac magis moveatur ad exorandam divinam eandemque immensam Dei benignitatem et Clementinam, quo vestram Reverendissimam amplitudinem tueatur, augeat et beet in aeternum. Amen." The names of the designated friars were then to be written at the end.

[49] Cf. Schmalzgrueber, *Ius Ecclesiasticum Universum,* lib. V, tit. 38, n. 32.

[50] Const. *Etsi mendicantium,* 16 maii 1567—*Bull. Rom. Taur.*, VII, 573-584.

[51] Const. *Romani Pontificis,* 6 aug. 1571—*Fontes,* n. 139.

[52] 4 febr. 1622, § 1—*Fontes,* n. 199.

holding a parochial benefice or possessing episcopal approbation for hearing the confessions of seculars. A few years later Urban VIII (1623-1644) was even more explicit in his language than his predecessors. In a clear and forthright manner he decreed the abrogation of any and every indult enjoyed by Regulars and as granting the right to hear the confessions of seculars without any previous examination and approbation on the part of the ordinary. [53]

The jurisdiction of Regular confessors came from the Roman Pontiff. Since his diocese embraced the whole world, the reception of episcopal approbation enabled Regulars to hear the confessions of all secular penitents in the diocese in which they had been approved, even though the penitents came from another diocese. [54] There could arise of course the question whether such episcopal approbation was sufficient to enable a Regular to exercise papal jurisdiction anywhere, or whether the Regular was obliged to seek the approval of the bishop in each diocese in which he labored.

The occasion for a papal decision on this point presented itself in the year 1648. A dispute which had arisen in the West Indies between the bishop of the city of the Holy Angels and the Jesuits concerning the offices of preaching and of hearing confessions was submitted to the Holy See for a definitive judgment. Innocent X (1644-1655), the reigning pontiff, declared in his solution that Regulars, even those of the Society of Jesus, who had been approved by the bishop of one diocese to hear the confessions of seculars, could not hear such confessions in another diocese without the approbation of the bishop of this latter diocese. [55] A papal constitution promulgated by Clement X (1670-1676) in the year 1670 contained legislation to the same effect, [56] reiterating the necessity of episcopal approbation by the ordinary of the diocese in which the confessions were to be heard.

---

[53] Const. *Cum sicut,* 12 sept. 1628—*Fontes,* n. 208.

[54] Fagnanus, *Commentaria in Quinque Libros Decretalium* (5 libri in 3, Venetiis, 1729), lib. V. tit. *de poenitentiis et remissionibus,* c. "Omnis," n. 79 (hereafter cited *Commentaria*).

[55] Const. *Cum sicut,* 14 maii 1648, § 4, I, 9—*Fontes,* n. 232.

[56] Const. *Superna,* 21 iun. 1670, § 4—*Fontes,* n. 246.

As the general rule, then, episcopal approbation from the ordinary of the place where the confessions were to be heard was necessary in order that the Regular confessor might administer the sacrament of penance. It should be borne in mind, however, that such approbation did not necessarily imply the grant of jurisdiction. Confessors who belonged to an Order received their jurisdiction from the pope through their superiors. The latter acted as delegates of the Holy See, and thus conferred confessional jurisdiction on those of their subjects whom they judged competent for the office of hearing the confessions of the faithful.[57] In granting approbation the bishop could at the same time confer jurisdiction upon the Regular confessor. If he did so, and if the superior of the Regular had given his consent, then the jurisdiction of the confessor was twofold, papal and episcopal.

If the bishop conferred jurisdiction upon the Regular confessor and the superior was opposed to it, the confessor could impart absolution validly in virtue of such jurisdiction, but his action was illicit. This is evident from a response of the Sacred Congregation of Bishops and Regulars given in 1866.[58] The Sacred Congregation made it clear that a religious, though not approved according to the laws of his Order, could *validly* hear the confessions of seculars—even against the will of his superior—provided that he had faculties from the local ordinary. And this was true even when his Regular superior had suspended him from hearing the confessions of seculars; in this latter case the absolutions imparted by the Regular confessor were certainly bestowed illicitly, but just as surely not invalidly.

Since the papal privileges bestowed upon Regulars for the administration of the sacrament of penance were given immediately and directly to the Order and its superiors, and not directly to the individual religious, the Regular confessor who imparted absolution in virtue of faculties received from the bishop, but against the will of his superior,

---

[57] Laymann, *Theologiae Moralis in V libros partitae Liber V* (Venetiis, 1700), tract. VI, c. X, n. 19; Schmalzgrueber, *Ius Ecclesiasticum Universum*, lib. V, tit. 38 n. 44.

[58] S. C. Ep. et Reg., *Ordinis Praedicatorum*, 2 mart. 1866—*Acta Sanctae Sedis* (41 vols., Romae, 1865 - 1908), I (1865), 683-684.

lacked papal jurisdiction. Such a confessor could not absolve from reserved cases *in virtue of the papal privilege granted to the Orders of Regulars,* since he was functioning outside the pale of that privilege; in such instances his power over reserved cases depended upon the faculties he received from the bishop.

This completes the general view of the pre-Code legislation concerning Regular confessors and secular penitents when the latter did not belong to the household of the monastery. A few words must be added relative to those seculars who did belong to the household.

In its decree concerning the necessity of episcopal approbation for the act of hearing the confessions of seculars, the Council of Trent did not intend to include those seculars who belonged to a monastic household. This may be deduced from the fact that a later session of the same Council excluded from episcopal jurisdiction those seculars who belonged to the household of the monastery and were considered part of the family of Regulars. [59]

In the Constitution *Superna,* promulgated on June 21, 1670, Clement X (1670 - 1676) settled the disputes that had arisen as a result of the Tridentine legislation concerning the offices of preaching and of hearing confessions. In this Constitution the pontiff, among other things, declared that the Regular superiors and the Regular confessors of monasteries, or of colleges where the regular life was professed, could hear the confessions of seculars who lived there continuously as members of the household; he excluded those seculars who merely worked there. [60]

Regular confessors, therefore, needed only the approbation of their own superiors in order to hear the confessions of those secular persons who lived in their monasteries day and night and were subject to the Regulars, not by reason of the vow, but by reason of service. On the other hand, episcopal approbation was necessary when these confessors heard the confessions of seculars who merely worked in the monastery but lived outside of it. [61]

---

[59] Cf. sess. XXV, *de regularibus,* c. 11—Schroeder, *Canons and Decrees of the Council of Trent,* pp. 224, 492.

[60] Const. *Superna,* § 4—*Fontes,* n. 246.

[61] Cf. Fagnanus, *Commentaria,* lib. V, tit. *de poenitentiis et remissionibus,* c. "Omnis," n. 62; Ferraris, *Bibliotheca,* "approbatio," art. I, nn. 64-70.

ARTICLE 2. REGULARS AND RESERVED CASES

In the early days of their history the right of priests of the Mendicant Orders to hear confessions with the permission of the Holy See, its legates, or the local ordinary had been maintained by Clement IV (1265 - 1268), but with the understanding that such permission did not include the faculty to absolve from sins reserved to the Holy See, to its legates, or to the bishops.[62] When Martin IV (1281 - 1285) bestowed the broad grant of apostolic jurisdiction upon the Franciscans and upon the Dominicans, no such restriction was mentioned,[63] and apparently the priests of these Orders acted as though no such restriction was intended. The action taken by the French clergy at the court of Honorius IV (1285 - 1287) in the year 1286 presupposes that the friars were absolving from sins reserved to the bishops.[64]

The Constitution *Super cathedram,* promulgated by Boniface VIII (1294 - 1303) on February 18, 1300,[65] and renewed by Clement V (1305-1314) on May 9, 1312,[66] implied that no special faculty was granted to the friars to absolve from reserved sins. And this implication was reduced to an explicit statement in the year 1304; in that year Benedict XI (1303 - 1304) decreed that the Mendicants could not absolve from sins reserved to the Holy See or to the local ordinary, except in favor of penitents who were in danger of death.[67]

Clement V restored the Constitution *Super cathedram* of Boniface VII at the Council of Vienne (1311 - 1312). And at this very Council he forbade religious to absolve anyone from sins and censures reserved

---

[62] Const. *Quidam temere,* 20 iunn. 1265—*Bull. Francisc.,* III, 14; cf. *supra,* p. 18.

[63] Const. *Ad fructus vberes*—*Bull. Francisc.,* III, 480; cf. *Supra,* p. 18

[64] Cf. *supra,* p. 19.

[65] C. 2, *de sepulturis,* III, 6, in Extravag. com.; *Bull. Francisc.,* IV, 498; *supra,* p. 20.

[66] Const. *Dudum*—*c.* 2, *de sepulturis,* III, in Clem.; *Bull. Francisc.,* V, 87, n. 196[a]; *supra,* p. 21.

[67] Const. *Inter cunctas,* 17 febr. 1304—c. 1, *de privilegiis,* V, 7, in Extravag. com.; *Bull. Francis.,* V, 11; *supra,* pp. 20-21.

to the Holy See or to the local ordinary; religious who presumed to absolve from reserved excommunications as enacted by the general law or by provincial or diocesan statutes, unless they had received the faculty to do so from the general law or in virtue of a privilege, incurred automatically an excommunication reserved to the Holy See. The only religious for whom an exception was made in this decree were those who had received from the Apostolic See the privilege of administering the sacraments to members of their household or to the poor who lived with them as their guests. [68]

In the following century, however, faculties to absolve from reserved cases were explicitly granted to Regulars in the form of apostolic privileges. In the year 1436 Eugene IV (1431 - 1447) granted to the prelates of the Benedictine Congregation of the Observance of St. Justin, or to the monks appointed by them for the hearing of confessions, the faculties to hear the confessions of those who came to them, even apart from any and every permission on the part of the superiors of the penitents, and to absolve them from all sins and censures except those which were reserved to the local ordinaries or to the Holy See. [69] Two years later the same pontiff granted to the abbots of the Cistercians of the Regular Observance, and to the confessors appointed by them, the privilege to absolve from all sins and censures, except those which were reserved to the Holy See. [70]

Sixtus IV (1471-1484), in giving apostolic approval to the Order of Minims of St. Francis of Paula (1416-1507) in the year 1474, granted to the priests of the Order the privileges of hearing confessions in any diocese and of absolving from all sins, excommunications, suspensions, and interdicts reserved to the bishop either by the general law or by the bishop's specific act of reservation. [71] In 1516

[68] C. 1, *de privilegiis et excessibus privilegiatorum*, V, 7, in Clem.

[69] Const. *Regularem vitam*, § 16, 30 iun. 1436—*Bull. Rom. Taur.*, V, 25.

[70] Const. *Commissum*, 1438—Augustinus a Virgine Maria, *Privilegia omnium religiosorum Mendicantium et non Mendicantium* (3. ed., Lugduni, 1664), n. 20 (hereafter cited Augustinus).

[71] Const. *Sedes Apostolica*, 27 maii 1474— *Bull. Rom. Taur.*, V, 213-217. Julius II (1503-1513) confirmed this privilege in his Constitution *Dudum ad sacrum*, 28 iul. 1506—*Bull. Rom. Taur.*, V, 422-434.

Leo X (1513-1521) promulgated the Constitution *Dum intra*,[72] wherein he made it clear that the Mendicant friars had no power to absolve from the penalties that were inflicted *ab homine.*

The priests of the Society of Jesus received an extraordinary privilege in the year 1545. On July 3 of that year Paul III (1534-1549) imparted to them the privilege of absolving any of the faithful who approached them even with sins reserved to the *Holy See,* or with penalties and similarly reserved censures, a restriction being made solely with reference to the sins and penalties and censures mentioned in the "bull which is customarily read on Holy Thursday." [73]

The only exception in this broad faculty given to the Jesuits was any penalty or censure listed in the so-called *Bullae Coenae.* These were bulls issued by the various popes against heretics and schismatics, and had their origin probably about the beginning of the fourteenth century. They were all substantially the same, listing about twenty classes of excommunicated persons. Clement XIV (1769-1774) discontinued their issuance in 1769, but those that were already promulgated remained in force until Pius IX (1846-1878) brought forth the Constitution *Apostolicae Sedis* on October 12, 1869. [74]

This privilege was given to the Jesuits in the same year that the Council of Trent was opened. The Council itself, while it went into detail in its treatment of the penitential discipline of the Church, never expressly abrogated any privilege enjoyed by Regulars with regard to the absolution from reserved cases. [75] As a matter of fact, the Tridentine popes and their successors increased the content and the extension of these favors.

The faculties conceded to the Jesuits by Paul III contained one re-

---

[72] 19 dec. 1516—*Fontes,* n. 72; *supra,* p. 23.

[73] Const. *Cum inter cuntas*—Confettius, p. 151.

[74] Cf. Moriarity, *The Exarordinary Absolution from Censures.* The Catholic University of America Canon Law Studies, n. 113 (Washington, D. C.: The Catholic University of America 1938), p. 39. For an example of the list of censures contained in these bulls, confer Shuhler, *Privileges of Regulars,* p. 73, note 27.

[75] Shuhler, *Privileges of Regulars,* p. 75.

striction: the Jesuit confessors could not absolve from the sins and censures mentioned in the "*Bullae Coenae.*" Even this restriction, however, was partly ruled out in 1552 when Julius III (1550-1555) granted to the General of the Society of Jesus the faculty, to be exercised by him and by his successors either personally or through priests delegated by them, of absolving from sins of heresy and other sins against the faith and of absolving likewise from any censures resulting from such sins.[76] These two privileges were confirmed by Gregory XIII (1572-1585): in 1583, the privilege granted by Paul III;[77] in 1584, in and for the internal forum, for the whole world with the exception of Spain, the favor conceded by Julius III.[78]

The papal favors relative to confessional jurisdiction and absolution from censures had gradually become the common property of all Regulars, inasfar as they were capable of using them, through the canonical institution known as the inter-communication of privileges. In virtue of this "privilege of acquiring privileges," the Mendicant and non-Mendicant Regular confessor obtained the same papal jurisdiction and the same faculties to absolve from reserved cases.[79]

The period of prosperity enjoyed by Regulars with reference to their confessional privileges had begun to wane, and restrictions were being placed upon them.

In answer to a question proposed by St. Charles Borromeo, Archbishop of Milan, the Sacred Congregation of the Council stated on September 10, 1577, that the privileges granted to Regulars did not contain the faculty of absolving from those cases which the bishop had reserved to himself.[80] The Jesuits, however, as is evident from the declaration of Gregory XIII on March 10, 1579,[81] were not included

---

[76] Const. *Sacrae,* 1552—Augustinus, n. 62, p. 154; Shuhler, *Privileges of Regulars,* p. 74.

[77] Augustinus n. 59, pp. 152-153; Shuhler, *loc. cit.*

[78] Augustinus, n. 62. pp. 154-155.

[79] Cf. *supra,* Introduction, p. 7; Confettius, p. 294.

[80] Confettius, p. 367.

[81] Confettius, p. 367, nota.

in this decree of the Sacred Congregation. This reply showed the mind of the Holy See on the matter.

On January 9, 1601, the Sacred Congregation of Bishops and Regulars, at the command of Clement VIII (1592-1605), issued a decree binding upon all the priests in Italy, with the exception of Rome.[82] This was a declaration to the effect that no priest could, in virtue of confessional approbation, validly absolve from the following three types of cases: 1) from those clearly or even doubtfully recounted in the *Bullae Coenae*; 2) from those reserved in any way to the Holy See; and 3) from those reserved by the local ordinaries to themselves.

The following year the same Congregation promulgated a new decree similar to the preceding one, but containing a modification with reference to papal reservations.[83] The pontiff explicitly abrogated every privilege to absolve these cases that were reserved to the Holy See, regardless of how the privilege had been received or enjoyed. Priests, however, could absolve from papal cases not mentioned in this decree, in virtue of whatever privilege they had to do so. Moreover, since the prohibition to absolve from the reservations recounted in the decree of the year 1602, as in that of the year 1601, applied only to Italy, with the exception of Rome, Regular confessors in Rome itself and in the rest of the world could absolve even from the cases listed in the decree of 1602, excepted, of course, those recounted in the *Bullae Coenae*; and, even in reference to this last, they could, in virtue of their privilege, impart absolution from heresy.

Fifteen years later, Paul V (1605-1621) directed the Sacred Congregation of Bishops and Regulars to issue a decree which confirmed

---

[82] *Fontes*, n. 1596; cf. Shuhler, *Privileges of Regulars*, pp. 77.

[83] 26 nov. 1602—*Fontes*, n. 1616. By this decree, the following cases were reserved to the Holy See: cases (definitely) recounted in the *Bullae Coenae;* the violation of ecclesiastical immunity, as set forth in the Constitution *Cum alias nonnulli* of Gregory XIV; the violation of the cloister of nuns for an evil purpose; provocation to and participation in a duel, according to the decree of the Council of Trent and the Constitution *Ad tollendum* of Gregory XIII; the laying of violent hands on clerics, according to the canon of the II Lateran Council, *Si quis suadente*, etc.; real simony knowingly contracted, and confidential simony in relation to a benefice.

the fact that no priest, regardless of the privileges he enjoyed in the past, could absolve from cases reserved either to the local ordinaries or to the Holy See, in accordance with the legislation of Clement VIII.[84]

The preceding legislation, inasmuch as it was restricted to the confines of Italy, with the exception of Rome, was local. Nevertheless, it paved the way for a universal law. The mind of the Holy See was further revealed in the year 1665 when Alexander VII (1655-1667) condemned the proposition that Mendicants could absolve from cases reserved to the bishops without obtaining any special faculty from the bishops.[85]

Five years later, Clement X (1670-1676) enacted legislation that was binding throughout the Universal Church. In his Constitution *Superna,*[86] he enunciated the fundamental principle that Regulars could not, in virtue of their apostolic privileges, absolve from cases which the bishops had reserved to themselves. However, while the Regular confessor was unable, in the absence of a special faculty, to absolve from sins reserved in the diocese in which he was laboring, he could nevertheless absolve extra-diocesan penitents from sins reserved in their own diocese, provided that such sins were not reserved in the place where he was hearing confessions.

The sole exception to this latter regulation was illustrated in the phrase *"in fraudem reservationis."* In other words, the confessor was unable to grant absolution to such penitents if he knew that they had come to the strange diocese for the purpose of obtaining absolution.

The pope went on to state that Regulars who imparted absolution in virtue of papal privileges could not absolve from reserved cases in the external forum, but only in and for the internal forum. The bishop had the right to treat as one still under censure any penitent who had been absolved from the censure in virtue of a papal privilege.

[84] 7 ian. 1617—*Fontes,* n. 1684.

[85] S. C. S. Off., decr., 24 sept. 1665, § 1, n. 12: "Mendicantes possunt absolvere a casibus episcopis reservatis, non obtenta ad id episcoporum facultate."—*Fontes,* n. 734: DB, n. 1112.

[86] §§6-7, 21 iun. 1670—*Fontes,* n. 246.

The Clementine Constitution *Superna,* therefore, definitely established for the Universal Church the regulation that Regulars had no exceptional power to impart absolution from cases which the bishops had reserved to themselves, unless they had obtained a special faculty for that purpose. What were these "cases which the bishops had reserved to themselves?"

There were three types of cases reserved to the bishop: 1) Cases reserved by *episcopal statute,* whether in or outside a synod. Such reservations naturally depended upon the individual bishop, but among them were usually to be found such crimes as voluntary homicide, incendiarism, perjury at a trial, public adultery, falsification of letters, and the pollution of a church. 2) Cases reserved to the bishop in consequence of an *established recognized usage.* These depended upon the entrenched custom of the various dioceses. 3) Cases reserved to the bishop by the *common law.* Among these were included the following: striking a cleric, but not seriously; striking a cleric seriously, if committed by a woman; effectively procuring an abortion; participating in one and the same crime with persons excommunicated by the bishop.[87]

Of these three classes Regular confessors enjoyed the faculty of absolving from cases reserved to the bishops by custom or by the common law, but not from those which the bishops reserved to themselves by means of a personally enacted statute.[88]

The rights enjoyed by Regulars to absolve from cases reserved by the bishops to themselves were thus effectively rescinded by Clement X (1670-1676). The Regular confessor still retained, however, the a-

[87] Cf. Viva, *Cursus Theologico-moralis* (3. ed., 2 vols., Beneventi, 1737), II, pars 6, q. IX, art. II, ad VI, p. 129.

[88] Viva, *ibid.*, pars 8, q. 11, art. II, ad VII, p. 38. St. Alphonsus (1696-1787) admitted the probability of the opinion which maintained that Regulars could absolve even from those cases which the bishop had reserved to himself in a synod as long as he had not expressed them in writing; the non-incorporation of such cases in a written list gave rise to the presumption that the bishop wished to grant to all confessors the faculty of absolving from these cases.—St. Alphonsus Ligurori, *Theologia Moralis* (editio . . . nova . . . collata . . . recognita . . . illustrata, cura et studio P. Leonardi Gaudé, 4 vols., Romae: ex Typographia Vaticana, 1905-1912), lib VII, n. 100.

postolic privileges to absolve from cases reserved to the ordinary by the common law as well as to absolve from cases reserved to the Holy See.[89] One of these privileges was definitely revoked in the nineteenth century.

The year 1869 witnessed an important change in previous ecclesiastical legislation relative to *latae sententiae censures.* Accumulating over a period of years, their number had grown quite considerably; and the changing customs and times had rendered some of them useless. Aware of all this, Pius IX (1846-1878) brought forth a new and official list of automatic censures in the Constitution *Apostolicae Sedis,* which he promulgated on October 12, 1869.[90] All previously enacted censures, the incurring of which came automatically with the violation of the penal law, were abrogated if they were no longer listed in this Constitution. [91]

Pius IX divided the censures that were incurred automatically into six classes: (1) excommunications reserved to the Roman Pontiff in a special manner; (2) excommunications reserved to the Roman Pontiff in a simple manner; (3) excommunications reserved to the bishops or ordinaries; (4) excommunications not reserved to anyone; (5) suspensions reserved to the Roman Pontiff, and (6) reserved interdicts.

The Supreme Pontiff revoked any and all privileges Regulars had possessed up to that time in reference to censures reserved to the Holy See, whether they were reserved in a special manner or in a simple manner. [92] He did not abrogate the privileges possessed by Regular confessors to absolve from censures reserved to bishops or local ordinaries by the general law. "Since the *sententia communis* prior to the time of the Constitution *Apostolicae Sedis* maintained that Regular confessors could absolve in such cases, there is no doubt that

[89] Regulars in Italy, Rome excluded, could not absolve from the cases reserved to the Holy See in the decree of 1602; cf. *supra,* p. 33.

[90] *Fontes,* n. 552.

[91] Cf. Shuhler, *Privileges of Regulars,* p. 89.

[92] Const. *Apostolicae Sedis,* I, *post* n. 12; *ibid.,* VI, n. 2 *in medio*—*Fontes,* n. 552; Shuhler, *op. cit.,* p. 92.

there was sufficient probability of existence for the privilege after 1869 to make its use lawful and valid."[93]

The automatic censures reserved to the bishops or ordinaries by the Constitution of Pius IX were three: (1) excommunication incurred by clerics in sacred Orders, or by Regulars or nuns after their solemn vow of chastity, if they presumed to contract marriage; the same penalty was likewise incurred by the other partner in the attempted contract; (2) excommunication incurred by those who effectively procured abortion; (3) excommunication incurred by those who knowingly used false apostolic letters or who co-operated in such a crime.[94]

Article 3. Regulars and the Confessions of Religious

Religious, in virtue of the privilege of exemption, were no longer subject to the jurisdiction of the local ordinary. They were, on the contrary, immediately subject to the Holy See, which governed them through their superiors. From the very nature of exemption, the local ordinary possessed no power to grant faculties to a priest to absolve religious; such power was proper to the religious superior as the delegate of the Holy See. Hence a religious could confess validly only to his superior or to a priest delegated by the superior.[95]

Wherever the Benedictine Rule was adopted, either in its entirety or partially, the monks confessed to their abbot or to the priests delegated to him.[96] A similar procedure was followed by the members of the Mendicant Orders inasmuch as they had to confess their sins to priests who belonged to their own Order.[97] In the year 1265

[93] Shuhler, *op. cit.*, p. 95; cf. also *ibid.*, pp. 93-95.

[94] Const. *Apostolicae Sedis.* III—*Fontes,* n. 552.

[95] Cf. Shuhler, *Privileges of Regulars,* pp. 42-44.

[96] McCormick, *Confessors of Religious,* The Catholic University of America Canon Law Studies, n. 33 (Washington, D. C.: The Catholic University of America, 1926), pp. 10-11.

[97] *Ibid.*, pp. 12-15.

Clement IV (1265 - 1268) forbade the Franciscans to confess to any priests other than their superiors or the priests of their own Order, unless urgent necessity dictated otherwise.[98] A later pope, Benedict XI (1303 - 1304), granted broad confessional faculties to the Mendicants, but in conceding this privilege he explicitly excluded from their jurisdiction those religious who were obliged to confess their sins to their own superiors or who were forbidden by their superiors to confess to other priests.[99]

Such legislation, while certainly an important factor in furthering the observance of the religious life, could very easily be the ocassion of considerable difficulties. On October 17, 1404, Innocent VII (1404 - 1406) allowed Dominican priests to confess their sins to any regular or secular priest who was fit[100] for the hearing of confessions, if they were living outside their monastery for a legitimate reason and did not have at hand a suitable confessor of their own Order.[101] A similar privilege was granted to the Franciscans on August 11, 1479, by Sixtus IV (1471 - 1484).[102]

Even before the Council of Trent was convened, all the Mendicants, in virtue of the acknowledged intercommunication of privileges among

---

[98] Const. *Virtute conspicuos,* 21 iul. 1265, n. 24—*Bull. Rom. Taur.. III.* 741.

[99] Const. *Inter cunctas,* 17 febr. 1304—*Bull, Francisc..* V, 11; cf. *supra*, p. 21

[100] Pope Innocent used the phrase "*presbyterum idoneum.*" This raised the question whether the priest confessor had to be one legitimately approved by some ordinary. Shuhler (*Privileges of Regulars,* pp. 48-49) defends the more common opinion which answers the above question in the negative. Among those who take the affirmative position is Mocchegiani, *Iurisprudentia Ecclesiastica,* I, nn. 1013-1014. For a complete presentation and discussion of the problem, confer Mocchegiani, *ibid.,* nn. 1008-1014.

[101] Const. *Provenit*—Confettius, p. 26; Ferraris, *Bibliotheca,* "approbatio," art. II, n. 9; Shuhler, *Privileges of Regulars,* pp. 46-50. From the text of this constitution as recorded in Confettius (*loc. cit.*) and as cited by Mocchegiani (*Iurisprudentia Ecclesiastica,* I, n. 1008) it is evident that Innocent VII granted this privilege to the Dominicans alone, and not to the Dominicans and Franciscans, as is maintained by Shuhler, *op. cit.,* p. 46.

[102] Const.*Supplicari nobis*—Confettius, p. 65; Ferraris, *loc. cit.;* Mocchegiani, ibid., n. 1008.

the Mendicant Orders, had shared in these papal favors; and the Council of Trent made no change in the existing legislation governing the confessions of Regulars.

It was Clement VIII (1592 - 1605) who set forth the regulation that the religious superior was obliged to appoint two or more confessors to hear the confessions of his subjects, and that a superior could lawfully hear the confessions of his subjects *only when* there was question of a reserved sin, or when the subjects voluntarily asked to go to confession to the superior.[103]

To hear the confessions of their own co-religious, then, Regulars needed only the approbation of their own superiors, not that of the bishop. They could also hear the confessions of the members of another Order, provided that the penitents had received from their own superiors the power to choose a confessor outside the Order to which they belonged.[104]

While a Regular, if on a journey or if living outside his monastery for a legitimate reason, could confess his sins to a priest who was not a member of his Order, he could not by the same token receive absolution from sins reserved in his own institute, unless some special statute gave him a privilege to the contrary. Hence, in the absence of any such particular law, Regular confessors could have absolved penitents of another Order only *indirectly* from sins reserved therein; the penitent would have been bound to repeat such a sin to his own superior or to another priest having the faculty to absolve from it.[105]

With reference to the confessors of nuns, the Council of Trent made no mention of the necessity of episcopal approbation. The proper superior supplied their confessor and gave him his jurisdiction:

---

[103] Decr. *Sanctissimus,* 26 maii 1593—*Fontes,* n. 177.

[104] Ferraris, *Bibliotheca,* "approbatio," art II, nn. 1, 15-16.

[105] Because of the burden involved in confessing the same sin twice, pre-Code authors excused such a penitent from confessing a reserved sin to a priest who lacked faculties to absolve from sins reserved in the penitent's Order. Cf. Lyszczarczyk, *Compendium Privilegiorum Regularium praesertim Ordinis Fratrum Minorum* (Leopoli, 1906), p. 136.

hence, the bishop, in the case of nuns subject to himself; the Regular superior, in the case of nuns subject to his jurisdiction.[106]

Gregory XV (1621 - 1623), however, introduced new legislation with reference to the confessors of nuns. In the Constitution *Inscrutabili,* promulgated on February 5, 1622,[107] the pontiff decreed that every ordinary or extraordinary confessor of nuns needed episcopal jurisdiction to hear their confessions, even if the nuns were subject to Regulars.

In the year 1670 Clement X (1670 - 1676) repeated this legislation. He stated clearly that a general approbation from the bishop to hear the confessions of seculars did not suffice for the act of hearing the confessions of nuns, and that a special approbation was necessary for religious to hear the confessions of nuns subject to them. Moreover, the special approval to hear the confessions of nuns in one monastery did not therby confer jurisdiction to hear the confessions of those in another.[108]

The legislation determining the necessity of episcopal approbation for any priest to hear the confessions of nuns was approved by Benedict XIV (1740-1758). In the Constitution *Ad militantis,* promulgated on March 30, 1742,[109] he forbade major tribunals to receive any appeals in matters which touched the examination for the approbation or the rejection of confessors for the act of hearing the confessions of nuns, even if the latter were subject to Regulars.

On December 11, 1758, Clement XIII (1758 - 1769) confirmed a decree of the Sacred Congregation of the Council to the effect that confessors of exempt nuns needed special approbation to exercise their function; that Regular confessors, approved specially by the bishop for one monastery of nuns or for one occasion, were not to be considered approved for all monasteries of nuns or for all occasions; and finally, that Regulars, in order to obtain faculties for hearing the

---

[106] McCormick, *Confessors of Religious,* p. 84.

[107] *Fontes,* n. 199.

[108] Const. *Superna,* § 4, 21 iun. 1670—*Fontes,* n. 246.

[109] § 20—*Fontes,* n. 326.

confessions of nuns or of seculars, were obliged to present themselves personally before the bishop.[110]

Up until the sixteenth century the members of approved religious institutes professed solemn vows. In the sixteenth and succeeding centuries new religious communities arose, communities whose members professed simple vows. In the beginning the Holy See at most tolerated these Congregations after their foundation, but later practically adopted a policy of not approving new religious foundations unless they were Congregations of simple vows. Complete pontifical approval was given to such institutes by Leo XIII (1878-1903) in the Constitution *Conditae a Christo,* promulgated on December 8, 1900.[111]

Religious of simple vows enjoyed greater freedom in going to confession than Regulars did. True, such religious had their appointed confessors, but in general they could confess validly to any priest approved for the hearing of confessions.[112] Regulars, on the other hand, were still bound by the general law of confessing their sins to designated priests. In the course of time, however, the confessional discipline for Regulars was relaxed.

Complete liberty to confess to a priest outside the Order or Congregation was granted in the year 1913. In February of that year Pius X (1903-1914) granted to all confessors in Rome, if duly appointed by the local ordinary, the faculty of absolving any religious penitent. On August 5, 1913, this privilege was extended to all confessors throughout the world who were approved by the local ordinaries.[113] All religious of whatever Order or Congregation, regard-

---

[110] Const. *Inter multiplices,* §§5-6—*Fontes,* n. 449; McCormick, *Confessors of Religious,* p. 87.

[111] Cf. Vermeersch, *De Religiosis Institutis et Personis: Supplementa et Monumenta* (2 vols., Vol. I, 2. ed., 1907; Vol II, 3. ed., 1904, Brugis), I, n. 57; Vermeersch, *op. cit.,* I, nn. 476-477.

[112] Cf. Vermeersch, *op. cit.,* I, nn. 476-477.

[113] S. C. de Religiosis, decr. *In audientia,* 5 aug. 1913—*Acta Apostolicae Sedis* (Romae: Typis Polyglottis Vaticans, 1909—), V (1913), 431 (hereafter cited *AAS*); cf. Schuhler, *Privileges of Regulars,* p. 59.

less of their sex, could confess their sins to any priest approved by the local ordinary for the act of hearing confessions. In such a case the confessor did not need the permission of the superior of the penitent religious. Moreover, the confessor could validly and licitly absolve the penitent from sins reserved in the Order or Congregation, even if such sins were reserved under censure.

HISTORICAL SUMMARY

Prior to the thirteenth century Regular confessors were, as a rule, subject to the local ordinary for their faculties to absolve secular penitents. History bears witness to the fact that in certain instances Regulars exercised papal jurisdiction in this matter, but this was the exception.

With the rise of the Mendicant Orders in the thirteenth century, papal jurisdiction was given more generally to religious confessors in the form of a privilege. The broadest grant of such a jurisdiction was bestowed by Martin IV (1281 - 1285) upon the Franciscans in the year 1281 and upon the Dominicans in the year 1282.

Since the thirteenth century, restrictions were gradually placed upon the exercise of this papal jurisdiction, restrictions that finally culminated in the decree of the Council of Trent (1545 - 1563), which made episcopal approbation mandatory for any priest who would hear the confessions of seculars.

The faculties to absolve from reserved cases, as granted to Regulars by the Roman Pontiffs, were partially revoked in post-Tridentine times. Whatever privileges Regulars possessed, namely, of absolving from cases which the bishops had reserved to themselves, were definitely revoked in the year 1670 by Clement X (1670 - 1676). In the year 1869 Pius IX (1846 - 1878) just as definitely abrogated any and all privileges they enjoyed in the matter of absolving from censures reserved to the Holy See. Regulars still retained, however, their privilege to absolve from censures reserved to the local ordinary by the general law.

Gregory XV (1621 - 1623) introduced legislation to the effect that episcopal approbation was required for the confessors of nuns. Clement X (1670 - 1676) added a further specification to this regulation by decreeing that a general episcopal approbation for hearing the confessions of seculars did not suffice for hearing those of nuns, but that special episcopal approbation was necessary.

The legislation concerning the confessions of religious gradually evolved to the point where all religious, including Regulars, enjoyed full liberty to seek absolution from any approved priest.

PART II

CANONICAL COMMENTARY

INTRODUCTION

When the Code of Canon Law made its initial appearance, the Church had already been in existence some nineteen hundred years. Throughout that long period of time she had been dealing with human beings, a fact which called for the exercise of her God-given legislative, judicial, and coercive powers. The Church's laws are never the result of whim or caprice; they are rather a definite expression on her part of her ardent desire to help her subjects attain the great purpose of life, namely, eternal salvation.

In those nineteen hundred years ecclesiastical laws have been many and varied; some have been abolished, others modified, new laws enacted. Keeping pace with her legal enactments has been the Church's constant desire to gather her legislation into a compact and unified form, a desire which inspired many churchmen during the course of the centuries to edit collections of canon law. In time these were multiplied to such an extent that everywhere the need for a single official collection was felt. The greatest step toward the practical realization of this need was taken by Pius X (1903 - 1914), who instituted the project for the new codification on March 19, 1904. The Code was promulgated in the pontificate of his successor, Benedict XV (1914 - 1922), on Pentecost Sunday, May 17, 1917.[1]

The faculties of Regular confessors rest on two basic canons in the Code of Canon Law, namely canons 874 and 875. The former of these deals with the jurisdiction delegated by the local ordinary, while the latter treats of the jurisdiction delegated by the religious superior. In addition to, and dependent upon, the delegated jurisdiction, Regular confessors enjoy certain powers in virtue of apostolic privileges.

---

[1] Const. *Providentissima Mater Ecclesi—Codex Iuris Canonici* (Romae: Typis Polyglottis Vaticanis, 1917), xxv-xxviii.

CHAPTER II

ORDINARY FACULTIES

ARTICLE 1. THE REGULAR CONFESSOR AND JURISDICTION DELEGATED BY THE LOCAL ORDINARY

Canon 874, § 1, sets forth a fundamental principle in relation to confessional jurisdiction. According to this canon, delegated jurisdiction to hear the confessions of any penitent at all, whether secular or religious, is conferred upon both secular and religious priests, even though the latter be exempt, by the ordinary of the place in which the confessions are heard; religious priests, however, are not to make use of this jurisdiction without at least the presumed permission of their superior, except in the case for which provision has been made in canon 519.[1]

Since good order demands that the local ordinary be prudent in grantng diocesan faculties, these should be given only to priests who are known to be worthy. In the case of religious priests, the superior should know his subjects better than the local ordinary. Hence the Code admonishes the latter not to grant confessional jurisdiction habitually to religious who are not presented to him by their proper superior.[2]

---

1 Canon 874, § 1: Iurisdictionem delegatam ad recipiendas confessiones quorumlibet sive saecularium sive religiosorum confert sacerdotibus tum saecularibus tum religiosis etiam exemptis Ordinarius loci in quo confessiones excipiuntur; sacerdotes autem religiosi eadem ne utantur sine licentia saltem praesumpta sui Superioris, firmo tamen praescripto can. 519.

2 Canon 874, § 2: Locorum Ordinarii iurisdictionem ad audiendas confessiones habitualiter ne concedant religiosis qui a proprio Superiore non praesentantur; iis vero qui a proprio Superiore praesentantur, sine gravi causa eam ne denegent, firmo tamen praescripto can. 877.

In the pre-Tridentine period Regular confessors, in virtue of the legislation of Boniface VIII (1294 - 1303),[3] had to be presented by their superiors to the bishop and the permission of the latter sought in order that they might exercise confessional jurisdiction. This law was further developed by the decree of the Council of Trent (1545 - 1563),[4] which imposed upon Regulars the necessity of receiving the approbation of the bishop before they could hear the confessions of secular penitents. While there is certainly no good reason to conclude that the bishops did not confer jurisdiction together with approbation, it was commonly held, before the Code, that the jurisdiction for Regulars relative to secular penitents was derived from the pope.[5]

These ideas of presentation and approbation are retained in the Code, with, however, one further significant development. In canon 874 the local ordinary confers not approbation in the sense commonly understood prior to the Code, but jurisdiction itself. Hence the wording of the present law apparently puts an end to the question whether Regulars received their jurisdiction for hearing the confessions of seculars from the Roman Pontiff or from the bishop by whom they were approved.[6] The text of canon 874 does not even use the word *approbation;* the local ordinary himself gives the necessary jurisdiction. As a mattter of fact, there can be no doubt that the meaning of approbation has undergone a modification in the Code. With reference to the sacrament of penance, the words *approbation* and *jurisdiction* can now be used synonymously; in this matter, when the Code speaks of approbation it refers to the possession of jurisdiction.[7] A glance at

---

[3] Const. *Super cathedram,* 18 febr. 1300—*Bull. Francisc.,* IV, 498-500; *supra,* p. 20.

[4] Sess. XXIII, *de ref.,* c. 15; *supra,* pp. 23-24.

[5] Cf. *supra,* pp. 24, 27.

[6] Cf. Pejska, *Ius Canonicum Réligiosorum* (3. ed., Friburgi Brisgoviae: Herder, 1927), p. 292.

[7] Cf. Kelly, *Jurisdiction of the Confessor* (New York: Benziger, 1928), p. 41; Motry, *Diocesan Faculties according to the Code of Canon Law,* The Catholic University of America Canon Law Studies, n. 16 (Washington, D. C.: The Catholic University of America, 1922), p. 96.

canon 905, which gives to the faithful the right to confess their sins to a confessor legitimately *approved,* justifies this conclusion.[8]

It is to be noted that *as a general rule* the immediate source of the jurisdiction of the Regular confessor, as far as the confessions of seculars are concerned, is the local ordinary and not the Roman Pontiff. However, the local ordinary cannot be the sole source. This is evident from the fact that Regular confessors enjoy certain powers in virtue of apostolic privileges, such as the privilege to dispense from certain private vows, to dispense from irregularities, and to absolve from those automatic censures which are reserved by the general law to the local ordinary.[9] In these matters the jurisdiction is granted, not by the local ordinary, but by the Roman Pontiff through the Regular superiors. The jurisdiction granted by the local ordinary at the present time here serves in much the same capacity as did episcopal approbation prior to the Code: the jurisdiction of the local ordinary is a necessary condition for the exercise of these papal privileges.

The necessity of episcopal approbation, therfore, has been modified to the necessity of delegated jurisdiction from the local ordinary relative to the confessions of secular penitents.

The Code indicates that a definite procedure is to be followed before the religious priest receives from the local ordinary delegated jurisdiction for the act of hearing confessions.[10]

First of all, the religious is to be presented by his proper superior. This is the general rule, inasmuch as the local ordinary is forbidden to grant jurisdiction habitually to religious who are not presented by their proper superior.[11]

Secondly, the fitness of the religious must have been proved by means of an examination. The local ordinary is forbidden to confer

---

[8] Canon 905: Cuivis fideli integrum est confessario legitime approbato etiam alius ritus, cui maluerit, peccata sua confiteri.

[9] The privilege to dispense from such censures is discussed and explained in Chapter IV of this dissertation.

[10] Cf. Pejska, *Ius Canonicum Religiosorum,* pp. 293-294.

[11] Canon 874, § 2.

jurisdiction upon a priest unless the latter has been proved suitable by means of an examination.[12] The local ordinary, however, need not conduct this examination himself. Religious superiors, either personally or through the members of the theological faculty, generally examine the fitness of the religious priest for the active ministry.[13] No examination is necessary if the theological learning of the priest is known from some other source.[14] In any event, the local ordinary can accept the testimony of the religious superior concerning the fitness of the priest presented for faculties.[15]

Thirdly, the priest must make the profession of faith before the local ordinary or his delegate.[16] The general law of the Church does not oblige a priest who has made the profession of faith preparatory to the reception of confessional faculties in or for one diocese to repeat it in another diocese.[17] The religious superior can be delegated by the local ordinary to receive this profession of faith.[18]

Fourthly, the actual delegation of jurisdiction to hear confessions must be given expressly either orally or in writing.[19] The jurisdiction is granted expressly if it is conferred either explicitly or implicitly. The necessary faculties to hear confessions are granted implicitly whenever the local ordinary, for example, invites a Regular to preach a mission to the faithful or to give a retreat for the clergy or religious

---

[12] Canon 877, § 1.

[13] Augustine, *A Commentary on the New Code of Canon Law* (8 vols.: Vols. I-II, 6. ed., 1931-1936; Vols. III, V, 5. ed., 1938; Vols. IV, VI-VIII, 3. ed., 1925-1931, St. Louis: Herder, 1925-1938), IV, 263.

[14] Canon 877, § 1.

[15] Cf. Pejska, *op. cit.*, p. 294.

[16] Canon 1406, § 1, 7^{0}: Coram loci Ordinario eiusve delegato, (obligatione emittendi professionem fidei, secundum formulam a Sede Apostolica probatam, tenentur) ... sacerdotes confessionibus excipiendis destinati ... antequam facultate donentur ea munia exercendi.

[17] Cf. Coronata, *Institutiones Iuris Canonici* (2. ed., 5 vols., Taurini: Marietti, 1939-1947), II, 350 (hereafter cited *Institutiones*). Cf. also Wernz-Vidal, *Ius Canonicum*, IV, ii, 23, nota 41.

[18] Canon 1406, § 1, 7^{0}: Pejska, *loc. cit.*

[19] Canon 879, § 1.

in his diocese, even though he makes no mention of the grant of jurisdiction in his letter of invitation.[20] Again, the grant of delegated jurisdiction is implied when a visiting Regular is appointed for confessional duty by a superior who has received from the local ordinary the faculty to confer such jurisdiction.

In virtue of canon 874, § 1, then, the local ordinary by granting jurisdiction empowers any Regular priest to absolve secular penitents and religious. The use of such faculties by the Regular confessor is always valid. For their licit use he must have the permission of his superior; presumed permission will suffice. The Regular can generally presume this permission if there is no evidence that the will of his superior is opposed to it.[21]

To this need of permission for licitness the law itself constitutes canon 519 as an exception. If a religious, even an exempt religious, for peace of conscience goes to a Regular confessor who has jurisdiction from the local ordinary, that confession is valid and licit, and the confessor can absolve the penitent religious even from sins and censures reserved in the latter's religious institute.[22] Any act or command, therefore, of a religious superior, by which one of his subjects is forbidden to hear the confession of another, is for the time being withdrawn, for all practical purposes, when the foregoing conditions are verified.

It is to be noted that the power granted by the general law in canon 519 to this occasional confessor for male religious, in virtue

---

[20] Cf. Coronata, *De Sacramentis Tractatus Canonicus* (3 vols., Taurini-Romae: Marietti, 1943-1946), I, 352 (hereafter cited *De Sacramentis*).

[21] Cf. "De confessione sacramentali in ordine nostro"—*Acta Ordinis Fratrum Minorum* (Ad Claras Aquas: ex Typographia Collegii S. Bonaventurae, 1889—), LXI (1942), 46.

[22] Canon 519: Firmis constitutionibus quae confessionem statis temporibus praecipunt vel suadent apud determinatos confessarios peragendam, si religiosus, etiam exemptus, ad suae conscientiae quietem, confessarium adeat ab Ordinario loci approbatum, etsi inter designatos non recensitum confessio, revocato quolibet contrario privilegio, valida et licita est; et confessarius potest religiosum absolvere etiam a peccatis et censuris in religione reservatis.

of which he can absolve from sins and censures reserved in the religious institute, does not include the faculty to absolve from any case *reserved by the general law* to the local ordinary, to the religious superior, or to the Holy See, nor does it include the power to absolve from any *ab homine* reserved sin, or from a censure inflicted *ab homine* in a particular case.[23] Nor can the confessor, in virtue of canon 519 alone, absolve *non-exempt* religious from any sins and censures *reserved by diocesan law.*[24] Once, however, the jurisdiction of the local ordinary has been obtained, the confessor who absolves a religious under canon 519 can invoke canon 2254 to grant absolution from any reserved automatic censure, and canon 900, under the circumstances stated therein, to absolve from reserved sins. Regular confessors can absolve their penitents from those automatic censures which are reserved to the local ordinary by the general law.[25]

Can the Regular confessor who has received jurisdiction from the local ordinary alone absolve an *exempt* religious from sins and censures which that local ordinary has reserved to himself? There is no problem with reference to the censures reserved by the local ordinary. In the first place, Regulars, and those who share the privilege of exemption with them,[26] are exempt from the jurisdiction of the local ordinary except in those matters concerning which the law specifically states that they are not exempt.[27] It is true that the local ordinary can punish or coerce religious in those matters in which they are subject to him;[28]

---

[23] Beste, *Introductio in Codicem* (2. ed., Collegeville, Minn.: St. John's Abbey Press, 1944), 339-340 (hereafter cited *Introductio*); cf. Berutti, *Institutiones Iuris Canonici* (6 vols. Vols. I, III et VI, Taurini-Romae: Marietti, 1936-1938), III, n. 39, ad VI.

[24] Cf. Berutti, *loc cit.*

[25] Cf. Chapter IV of this disseration.

[26] The Redemptorists and the Passionists, although not Regulars enjoy the privilege of exemption. Cf. Schaefer, *De Religiosis* (3. ed., Roma: S.A.L.E.R., 1940), p. 794, nota 85.

[27] Canon 615: Regulares, novitiis non exclusis, sive viri sive mulieres, cum eorum domibus et ecclesiis, exceptis iis monialibus quae Superioribus regularibus non subsunt, ab Ordinarii loci iurisdictione exempti sunt, praeterquam in casibus a iure expressis.

[28] Canon 619

in such instances they can incur a censure if one has been enacted. However, it may be stated that generally censures enacted by the bishop are concerned with the faithful at large and do not extend to those things in which exempt religious are subject to him.[29] Accordingly they would not incur such a censure. In the second place, a censure directly affects the penitent, not the confessor; hence, if the censure has not been incurred, the confessor can grant absolution from the sin.

There is a problem, however, with reference to the simple episcopal reservation, that is, the reservation of a sin *ratione sui,* not *ratione censurae.* Can the confessor, with jurisdiction from the local ordinary and without any special faculty over reserved sins, absolve an *exempt* religious from a sin reserved by that local ordinary? Coronata maintains that he can.[30] The majority of the authors claims that he cannot.[31]

The solution of the problem depends upon the source of the jurisdiction in canon 519. Is the jurisdiction which is exercised by the occasional confessor over exempt religious derived directly and immediately from the Roman Pontiff, or from the local ordinary?[32] If the opinion which maintains that the jurisdiction flows directly from the pope, or the general law itself, is correct, then the jurisdiction

---

[29] Cf. Voltas, "De reservatione episcopali quoad regulares"—*Commentarium pro Religiosis* (Romae, 1920—; ab anno 1935: *Commentarium pro Religiosis et Missionariis*), III (1922), 72 (hereafter cited *CpR* and *CpRM* respectively).

[30] *Institutiones,* I, 676, nota 4.

[31] Such is the opinion of Goyeneche, *Iuris Canonici Summa Principia,* Pars II, *De Religiosis* (Romae: Tip. Pol. "Cuore di Maria," 1938), n. 27, nota 19; Cappello, *Tractatus Canonico-Moralis de Sacramentis* (3 vols. in 6, Romae: Marietti, 1935-1945. Vol. III, Partes I et II, *De Matrimonio,* 4. ed., 1939; vol. II, De Poenitentia, 4. ed. 1944), II, n. 371. (hereafter cited *De Sacramentis*); Voltas, "De reservatione episcopali quoad regulares"—*CpR,* III (1922), 77; Larraona, "Commentarium"—*CpR,* X (1929), 366; Creusen, III (1922), 77; Larraona, "Commentarium—*CpR,* X (1929), 366; Creusen, *Religious Men and Women in the Code* (4. Eng. ed., revised and edited to conform with the 5. French edition, by Adam C. Ellis; first translation by Edward F. Garesché, Milwaukee: Bruce, 1940), n. 108; Aertnys-Damen, *Theologia Moralis* (14. ed., 2 vols., Torino: Marietti, 1944). II, n. 388.

[32] Coronata, *Institutiones,* I, 676, nota 4; cf. Larraona, "Commentarium" —*CpR,* X (1929), 254, nota 22; 362, nota 68; and 366, nota 85.

conferred by the local ordinary is rather, in this particular instance envisioned by canon 519, an approbation necessary for the exercise of papal jurisdiction. The reservation of a sin *ratione sui,* which is a limitation placed on the jurisdiction of the confessor, would thus have no effect in limiting jurisdiction derived immediately from the Sovereign Pontiff. And since the confessor's power cannot be limited in this particular case by an episcopal reservation, and since *exempt* religious, in virtue of the privilege of exemption, are not subject to the reservations made by the local ordinary, there seems no reason why the confessor who exercises the jurisdiction granted in canon 519 cannot absolve an exempt religious from any sin reserved *ratione sui* by the local ordinary.[33]

Such a conclusion is indeed warranted if the premises of the argument are true. However, they seem to be false. The local ordinary enjoys ordinary jurisdiction for the hearing of confessions in his territory.[34] According to canon 874, § 1, the local ordinary can *delegate*—not *subdelegate*—any priest to hear the confessions of *any one at all* in his territory. In canon 519, the confessor enjoys a jurisdiction delegated by the local ordinary who, in turn, possesses that jurisdiction as one of his *ordinary* powers.[35] In granting delegated jurisdiction the local ordinary may impose certain restrictions for a reasonable cause.[36] Such a restriction is the reservation of sins, because this places a limitation on the jurisdiction of the confessor. And this limited jurisdiction is the only jurisdiction exercised by the confessor who absolves a religious, exempt or non-exempt, in virtue of canon 519. The general law suspends exemption as far as the confessional jurisdiction of the local ordinary or his delegate and such an exempt penitent religious are concerned.[37]

---

[33] Cf. Coronata, *loc. cit.;* Larraona, *ibid.,* 366, nota 85.

[34] Canon 873, § 1: Ordinaria iurisdictione ad confessiones excipiendas... potiuntur...pro suo quisque territorio Ordinarius loci, et parochus....

[35] Cf Larraona, *op. cit.,* X (1929), 254, nota 22.

[36] Canon 878, § 1: Iurisdictio delegata aut licentia audiendarum confessionum concedi potest certis quibusdam circumscripta finibus.

§ 2. Caveant tamen locorum Ordinarii ac religiosi Superiores ne iurisdictionem aut licentiam sine rationabili causa nimis coarctent.

[37] Cf. Larraona, *op. cit.,* X (1929), 326, nota 68.

In virtue of the above presented intrinsic reasons and of the strong extrinsic authority,[38] it seems that the only correct view in this matter is that which maintains that a confessor who possesses jurisdiction from the local ordinary alone and who lacks any special faculty over reserved sins from the local ordinary cannot, in virtue of canon 519 alone, absolve an exempt religious who confesses to him a sin reserved by and to the local ordinary.

Of course, with reference to sins and censures reserved in the religious institute, the confessor's power comes not from the local ordinary or the religious superior, but from the law itself. In this case, it may be said that either the reservation ceases when canon 519 is employed, or the law itself grants the faculty to the confessor approved by the local ordinary.[39]

ARTICLE 2. THE REGULAR CONFESSOR AND JURISDICTION DELEGATED BY THE RELIGIOUS SUPERIOR

The right to grant confessional jurisdiction does not belong exclusively to the local ordinary. Together with him the proper religious superior of an exempt clerical institute shares this prerogative as far as the latter's own subjects are concerned. Canon 875, § 1, empowers such a superior to confer delegated jurisdiction for the act of hearing the confessions of the professed, of the novices, and of others who live in the religious house day and night as servants, guests, students, or because of ill health.[40] The particular law or constitutions

---

38 Cf. *supra*. p. 53, note 31.

39 Cappello, *De Sacramentis*, II, n. 305.

40 Canon 875, § 1: In religione clericali exempta ad recipiendas confessiones professorum, novitiorum aliorumve de quibus in can. 514, § 1, iurisdictionem delegatem confert quoque proprius eorundem Superior, ad normam constitutionum, cui fas eam concedere etiam sacerdotibus e clero saeculari aut alius religionis.

Canon 514, § 1: In omni religione clericale ius et officium Superioribus est per se vel per alium aegrotis professis, novitiis, aliisve in religiosa domo diu noctuque degentibus causa famulatus aut educationis aut hospitii aut infirmae valetudinis, Eucharisticum Viaticum et extremam unctionem ministrandi.

of each exempt clerical institute will determine what superior is competent to grant this jurisdiction. As a general rule it is not the local superior. [41]

The jurisdiction exercised by the religious superior over his subjects is personal. According to canon 502 the supreme moderator of a religious institute enjoys power over all the provinces, all the houses, and all the members of the institute; other superiors exercise a like power within the limits of their office. [42] Hence the local superior has jurisdiction over his own community, while the provincial enjoys the same power over the entire province. At the same time the exercise of such power in not restricted to the particular territory, but each superior can exercise it over his own subjects anywhere in the world. [43]

The ordinary jurisdiction possessed by superiors of exempt religious for the act of hearing the confessions of their own subjects is likewise personal; and it retains this characteristic even when it is delegated. [44] The confessor who is delegated by the competent religious superior of an exempt clerical institute exercises personal confessional jurisdiction over those subject to the delegating authority, and this without any restriction as to subjects or to territory unless such a limitation has been expressed in the grant of jurisdiction. Restrictions of this sort are not to be presumed or presupposed. [45]

There is an important difference, therefore, between the jurisdiction delegated by the local ordinary and that delegated by the religious superior. The former is territorial, while the latter is personal. The Regular confessor who absolves in virtue of diocesan faculties is restricted in their exercise to the territory of the diocese. The Regular confessor who absolves in virtue of jurisdiction granted to him by

---

[41] Schaefer, *De Religiosis*, n. 166, ad 3; Beste, *Introductio*, p. 339.

[42] Beste, *op. cit.*, p. 330; cf. Larraona, "Commentarium"—*CpR*. X (1929), 255, nota 26.

[43] Beste, *loc cit.*

[44] Cf. Coronata, *De Sacramentis*, I, 342; Aertnys-Damen, *Theologia Moralis*, II, n. 362.

[45] Cf. Larraona, *ibid.*, 255, nota 26; and 256, nota 33.

his superior is not limited territorially in their use; on the contrary, he can hear, anywhere in the world, the confessions of those subject to the particular superior who granted him the delegated jurisdiction.[46]

Hence in the Mendicant institutes and in others with a like organization, unrestricted jurisdiction granted to a Regular confessor by the supreme moderator or General of the institute empowers him to hear the confessions of the professed members and novices of the entire institute; in virtue of such delegated power he can, moreover, absolve those penitents who live day and night in any of the houses of the particular Order as candidates, servants, guests, students, or even for the sake of health. Since the jurisdiction of such a confessor is personal, he can absolve these penitents anywhere in the world. The same is true with reference to faculties delegated by the provincial and local superior,[47] except that the scope of the delegated jurisdiction is restricted to the province and to the local community respectively; in either case, however, the power of the confessor remains personal and can be exercised over the particular and assigned subjects anywhere in the world.

In contradistinction to the foregoing, the organization of the monastic institution—for example, the black Benedictine—follows a different pattern. While the various individual monasteries are self-sufficient and autonomous, they are sometimes rather loosely united into a congregation; these congregations themselves are likewise independent, each being ruled by its own constitutions, its own declarations on the rule, and its own superior. Finally, the congregations are united into a federation.[48]

---

46 Cf. Beste, *Introductio*, p. 339.

47 It is here supposed, of course, that the local superior is competent to grant jurisdiction. The Constitutions of the Order of Frairs Minor do not give the local superior the right to grant jurisdiction to the confessors to whom the friars are to confess regularly. Cf. *Regula et Constitutiones Generales Fratum Minorum* (Quaracchi: Ex Typographia Collegii S. Bonaventurae, 1922), n. 346. These Constitutions contain nothing expressly forbidding the local superior to grant jurisdiction to confessors to hear *occasionally* the confessions of his friars and other subjects; cf. Goyeneche, "Consultationes"—*CpR, VII* (1926), 40. According to Capobianco (*Privilegia*, n. 93), the local superiors of the Friars Minor cannot grant delegated jurisdiction to a confessor.

48 Beste, *Introductio*, pp. 327-328; cf. also Schaefer, *De Religiosis*, nn. 41 and 51 ad 7.

The abbots and conventual priors—that is, the superiors of the individual monasteries and priories respectively—can grant jurisdiction for hearing the confessions of those subject to them in the manner explained above.[49] The jurisdiction delegated to the Regular confessor is again personal; since this is so, he can absolve these subjects not only in the monastic house but anywhere in the world.

According to canon 518, § 1, in the individual houses of a clerical institute there are to be appointed several confessors, proportionate to the number of religious in the house; and in the case of an exempt institute, these confessors are to be invested with the faculty of absolving from cases reserved in the institute.

Of the confessors who have received jurisdiction from the competent religious superior, then, only those who have been designated for the confessions of the religious enjoy, in virtue of canon 518, § 1, the faculty to absolve from sins and censures reserved in the institute. The other confessors do not possess this power unless it is given to them by the delegating superior. Of course, if the confessor likewise possesses jurisdiction from the local ordinary, he can absolve from such cases in virtue of canon 519.

Nevertheless, from the viewpoint of the source of jurisdiction, it is evident that there is an important difference in the powers enjoyed by the confessor who has received his jurisdiction from the local ordinary alone, and by the confessor who has received his jurisdiction from the religious superior alone. In the first place, the confessor approved only by the local ordinary can absolve an exempt religious from cases reserved in the religious institute; the confessor approved by the superior cannot do so unless he is among those designated for the confessions of the religious, or unless the superior has granted him the power. In the second place, the confessor approved by the local

---

[49] Cf. Beste, *ibid.*, p. 339, nota 1. The constitutions of the particular congregation must be consulted if one is to determine whether or not the abbot president of the congregation can grant jurisdiction for the whole congregation. The abbot primate of the Benedictine Confederation cannot grant jurisdiction to a confessor for the whole Order. Cf. also Augustine, *A Commentary on the New Code of Canon Law*, IV, 259 and 266.

ordinary cannot absolve an exempt religious from sins reserved by the local ordinary; the confessor approved by the superior can absolve the subjects of that superior from sins reserved by the local ordinary.[50]

It very often happens that the Regular confessor is the recipient of a twofold delegation: both his own superior and the local ordinary confer jurisdiction upon him. In such a case the separate powers mentioned in the preceding paragraph coalesce in him. A few examples will clarify the meaning of this statement.

Let it be supposed that a certain sin is reserved by the bishop of Diocese X and that a sin of a different species is reserved in and by Religious Order Z. A priest who belongs to this Order receives provincial faculties from the competent superior, but without any special faculty to absolve from the sin reserved in the Order. The same Regular is granted diocesan faculties by the bishop of Diocese X, but likewise without any special faculty to absolve from the particular sin reserved in the diocese. The Regular is stationed in one of the houses of his province located in the above mentioned diocese.

A member of his own Order goes to confession to this Regular confessor and confesses a sin that is reserved in the religious institute. The confessor can absolve him, not in virtue of his provincial faculties, but in virtue of the ruling contained in canon 519, inasmuch as he has jurisdiction from the local ordinary. On a later occasion another member of his Order confesses a sin that is reserved in the diocese. The Regular confessor can absolve him, not in virtue of his diocesan faculties and the provision of canon 519, but in virtue of the provincial faculties which he has received from his superior; the sin reserved in the diocese has not been withdrawn from the jurisdiction of the confessor by his delegating superior. Now a member of his Order comes to the Regular confessor and in his confession accuses himself of a sin that is reserved in the diocese *and* of a sin reserved in the Order. The confessor can absolve him in virtue of the powers he has received from the twofold jurisdiction: the jurisdiction granted

---

[50] Cf. Aertnys-Damen, *Theologia Moralis,* II, n. 388; Coronata, *Institutiones,* I, 676, nota 4.

to him by his superior enables him to absolve the sin reserved in the diocese, while the jurisdiction from the local ordinary, in conjunction with canon 519, enables him to absolve the sin reserved in the religious institute.

The only instance in which the Regular confessor as here contemplated is incapable of imparting absolution to one of his confreres is that in which the sin reserved by the local ordinary and the sin reserved in the Order are identical. While it may be said that he can absolve the sin reserved in the Order because of the powers granted to him in canon 519, he evidently cannot absolve the sin reserved in the diocese by means of his provincial faculties inasmuch as the faculty to absolve from that particular sin has been withheld from him by the delegating superior.[51]

The jurisdiction thus delegated by the competent superior of an exempt clerical institute can be exercised by the confessor over those who live by day and night in the seminaries, colleges, schools, houses of hospitality, and hospitals that may be conducted by the religious of an exempt clerical institute. In such cases the jurisdiction from the local ordinary is not necessary, even though the subjects are members of the laity or members of another male religious institute.[52] For the exercise of this jurisdiction delegated by the religious superior a habitual residence is required on the part of the subjects. That is sufficient to include them within the scope of those who live "day and night" in the religious house.[53] The penitent can confess to the priest invested with this power even while on a journey, whether of lengthy or slight duration.[54]

[51] In the preceding examples only the ordinary circumstances have been taken into consideration. The faculty over reserved sins granted under the conditions in canon 900 has no place in the foregoing discussion.

[52] Cf. canon 875, § 1, together with canon 514, § 1.

[53] It should be noted, however, that the intention to stay in the religious house for at least a day and night is sufficient to invest the visitor with the right to make his confession there to a priest who possesses jurisdiction delegated by the competent superior, and to receive absolution from him. Cf. Shuhler, *Privileges of Regulars,* pp. 112-113.

[54] Cf. Larraona, "Commentarium"—*CpR.* X (1929), 256; Aertnys-Damen, *Theologia Moralis,* II, n. 363.

Once, however, the students or the guests or the others mentioned above have left the religious residence and have returned to their homes, the jurisdiction can no longer be exercised.[55] There seems no reason, though, why any one of these who has left just for a few days cannot confess to a priest with the proper faculties from the religious superior, even during the period of absence. Hence the Regular confessor can hear the confessions of those students, for example, who board at a seminary or other school conducted by his Order, and who at the present time are at home with their parents for a visit of a few days or even for a brief vacation.[56]

From these principles it follows that the Regular confessor can likewise absolve any of the penitents mentioned in the preceding paragraph from sins reserved in the diocese in which the confession is heard. In such instances the confessor can exercise the jurisdiction delegated by his religious superior.

Article 3. The Regular Confessor and the Confessions of Women Religious

The mere fact that a Regular confessor has received faculties from either his superior or the local ordinary does not give him the power to hear the confessions of women who are members of a religious institute. To hear such confessions validly he needs a *special jurisdiction,* granted by the ordinary of the place in which the house of the women religious is located.[57] Once again, however, the motherly solicitude of the Church for the welfare of her children is evidenced by the exceptions she provides to this general law. It is with these exceptions that the present article is concerned.

---

[55] Cf. Aertnys-Damen, *loc. cit.*

[56] Cf. Coronata, *De Sacramentis,* I, 342.

[57] Cf. Canons 876 and 525. To hear the confessions of the postulants the confessor does not need this *special* jurisdiction; jurisdiction from the local ordinary for hearing the confessions of women suffices. Cf. Coronata *Institutiones,* I. 678.

The Code contains provisions for six types of confessors of women religious: [58] 1) *the ordinary confessor,* who is appointed to hear the confessions of the community;[59] 2) *the special confessor,* who is appointed for a particular sister, [60] to be, as it were, her ordinary confessor; 3) *the extraordinary confessor,* who is appointed to hear the confessions of the community at least four times a year; [61] 4) *the supplementary confessor,* who is appointed as a sort of reserve for the community, and who can be summoned when necessary; [62] 5) *the occasional confessor* for any woman religious; [63] and 6) *the occasional confessor for women religious who are seriously ill.* [64]

The exceptions to the general law which requires special jurisdiction for the act of hearing the confessions of women religious embody the last two classes of confessors here listed. The occasional confessor in both these instances has neither special jurisdiction nor appointment from the local ordinary to hear confessions in a community of women religious. However, general jurisdiction from a local ordinary is at least required; the power delegated by the religious superior of an exempt clerical institute does not suffice.

According to canon 522, if a woman religious goes for peace of conscience to any confessor who is approved by the local ordinary for the confessions of women, and confesses to him in a church or in a public or semi-public oratory, her confession is valid and licit. [65] It matters not whether the penitent religious is professed or simply a

[58] Cf. Beste, *Introductio,* pp. 342-347; Raus, *Institutiones Canonicae* (Lugduni: Vitte, 1923), n. 181.

[59] Canon 520, § 1.

[60] Canon 520, § 2.

[61] Canon 521, § 1.

[62] Canon 521, § 2.

[63] Canon 522.

[64] Canon 523.

[65] Canon 522: Si, non obstante praescripto can. 520, 521, aliqua religiosa, ad suae conscientiae tranquillitatem, confessarium adeat ab Ordinario loci pro mulieribus approbatum, confessio in qualibet ecclesia vel oratorio etiam semipublico peracta, valida et licita est, revocato quolibet contrario privilegio....

novice. Novices likewise enjoy the privilege granted by this canon, since they are obliged by the same general law for confessors as are the women religious.[66] The peace of conscience postulated by the canon—which is by no means a condition necessary for the validity of the confession—is present when the religious wishes to make a sincere confession with the intention of receiving absolution.[67]

Three separate decisions of the Pontifical Commission for the Authentic Interpretation of the Code[68] have clarified the meaning of this canon. There is now no doubt that the religious when invoking the norm of canon 522 is given the option not only of personally approaching the confessor but also of summoning him for the confession she wishes to make; that her confession will be valid not only if it is made in a church or in a semi-public or public oratory, but likewise if it is made in any place legitimately destined for the confessions of women; that the place legitimately designated for the confessions of women may be designated particularly or for a special occasion, in accordance with the provisions of canon 910, § 1.

According to canon 909, § § 1 and 2, the confessional for women must always be placed in an open and conspicuous place, and generally in a church or in a public or semi-public oratory designated for women; moreover, between the confessor and the penitent there must be a fixed screen. The law, however, has foreseen the possibility of extraordinary cases, and has accordingly made provision for such cases in canon 910. The confessions of women are not to be heard outside the confessional unless such action is justified because of infirmity or any other true necessity; in these exceptions to the general rule any precautions decreed by the local ordinary must be used.[69]

---

[66] Canon 566, § 1: Cira sacerdotem a confessionibus in mulierum novitiatibus serventur praescripta can. 520-527.

[67] Beste, *Introductio*, pp. 341 and 344; cf. Creusen, *Religious Men and Women in the Code*, n. 118; Schaefer, *De Religiosis*, n. 176.

[68] 24 nov. 1920; 28 dec. 1927; 12 febr. 1935. Cf. Bouscaren, *The Canon Law Digest* (2 vols., Milwaukee: Bruce, 1934-1943), I. 295-296, and II, 161.

[69] Canon 910, § 1: Feminarum confessiones extra sedem confessionalem ne audiantur, nisi ex causa infirmitatis aliave verae necessitatis et adhibitis cautelis quas Ordinarius loci opportunas iudicaverit.

A Regular, called upon to fulfill the role of occasional confessor to a nun, sister, or novice, may find himself in various types of circumstances. The type of place where he is asked to hear the confession may range all the way from a chapel equipped with every modern confessional convenience to a parlor or room without benefit of any sort of confessional at all. Such a priest must remember that *the place* in which the confession is heard is a determinant of *the validty* of that confession.

The principles which he must keep in mind are these: in *ordinary* circumstances the choice of the place does *not* rest with the confessor or with the superioress or with the penitent herself; the choice of the place rests with the bishop or one who acts with authority from him, and in a place where *all* the prescriptions of the above-mentioned canon 909, § § 1 and 2, are duly observed. However, in *extraordinary* circumstances, in such, namely, as are envisioned in canon 910, §1, the confessor himself and the penitent may choose any particular place for this particular confession. In this latter instance, if the local ordinary has issued any instructions, the confessor must abide by them; if no instructions have been issued, the confessor is free to use his own discreet judgment.[70]

A Regular confessor, who would not hesitate to hear a women's confession outside the confessional because sickness on the part of the penitent or some true necessity on the part of either the penitent or himself justifies his action,[71] can, in like circumstances, validly and licitly hear the confession of a woman religious outside the confessional, even though there is no screen present.[72]

Thus far the occasional confessor for any woman religious has been the subject of discussion. Something must now be said about the occasional confessor for women religious who are seriously ill.

---

[70] Cf. canon 910, § 1; Beste, *op. cit.*, p. 346.

[71] For licitness, a woman's confession must be heard in some sort of confessional unless necessity dictates otherwise. Cf. canons 909, §§ 1 and 2, and 910, § 1; Connell, "The Place for a Woman's Confession"—*The American Ecclesiastical Review*, CXVIII (1948), 62-63.

[72] Cf. Bonzelet, *The Pastoral Companion* (9. ed., Chicago: Franciscan Herald Press, 1943), n. 50; Beste, *loc. cit.*

Canon 523, from which the powers of this confessor are deduced, states that all women religious, when they are gravely ill, even though there is no danger of death, can summon any priest at all who is approved for hearing the confessions of women, even though he is not designated for women religious, and during their grave illness they can confess to him as often as they wish.[73] Novices are included in the privilege of this canon.[74]

The canon itself expressly abstracts from the danger of death. For all practical purposes the sickness is to be considered grave if it could easily become dangerous; or if, because of her illness, the religious has to stay in bed for a week; or even if the religious has to undergo any sort of operation. In case of doubt the religious is to be favored and the confessor can act without scruple.[75]

There is a significant difference between the text of canon 522 and that of canon 523. While the former demands that the confessor be *approved by the local ordinary* for the confessions of women,[76] the latter merely requires that the confession be made to any priest *approved* for the confessions of women, and omits all mention of the local ordinary.[77] The source of the approval mentioned in canon 523 has given rise to a dispute among moralists and canonists.

Some authors claim that the occasional confessor for the religious who is gravely ill must have jurisdiction for the confessions of women from the ordinary of the place in which the confession is heard,[78] and

---

73 Canon 523: Religiosae omnes, cum graviter aegrotant, licet mortis periculum absit, quemlibet sacerdotem ad mulierum confessiones excipiendas approbatum, etsi non destinatum religiosis, arcessere possunt eique, perdurante gravi infirmitate, quoties voluerint confiteri....

74 Cf. canon 566, § 1; *supra*, p. 63.

75 Cf. Cappello, *De Sacramentis*, II, n. 317.

76 Canon 522: Si ... aliqua religiosa ... confessarium adeat ab Ordinario loci pro mulieribus approbatum ...

77 Canon 523: Religiosae omnes... quemlibet sacerdotem ad mulierum confessiones excipiendas approbatum... arcessere possunt....

78 E.g., Beste, *Introductio*, p. 347; Creusen, *Religious Men and Women in the Code*, n. 123.

they base their conclusion on the fact that delegated jurisdiction for the act of hearing confessions is conferred, according to canon 874, § 1, by the ordinary of the place in which the confessions are heard. Others maintain that jurisdiction granted by any local ordinary is sufficient for the exercise of the faculty granted in canon 523.[79] This second opinion is based both on canon 18, which states that laws are to be interpreted according to the proper meaning of the words taken in their text and context, and on the differences which exist between canons 522 and 523 and the decree *Cum de Sacramentalibus,*[80] upon which the former two canons are based.[81]

Wouters (1864 - 1933), who is quoted as holding this latter view,[82] evidently changed his opinion. In a later work[83] he maintained that this opinion seems contrary to the spirit of the law taken in its entirety, which constantly requires jurisdiction conferred by the ordinary of the place in which the confession is heard.[84] Aertnys-Damen, after briefly discussing the problem, state that the second opinion is not solidly probable, since it seems contrary to the intention of the legislator.[85] Other authors either do not raise the issue or merely take it for granted that the priest mentioned in canon 523 already

---

[79] E.g., McCormick, *Confessors of Religious,* pp. 225-229; Browne, *Handbook of Notes on Theology* (revised edition, St. Louis: Redemptorist Fathers, 1944), p. 32; Marc-Gestermann, *Institutiones Morales Alphonsianae* (17. ed., 2 vols., Lugduni: Vitte, 1922-1923), II, n. 1764 b.

[80] S. C. de Religiosis, 3 febr. 1913, nn. 14-15—*Fontes,* n. 4416.

[81] Cf. McCormick, *loc. cit.*

[82] McCormick, *op. cit.,* p. 228; Creusen, *loc. cit.*

[83] *Manuale Theologiae Moralis* (2 vols., Brugis: Beyaert, 1932-1933), II, n. 373 b.

[84] Wouters, *loc. cit*: "Cum canon [i.e. canon 523] edicat: *quemlibet sacerdotem, ad mulierum confessiones excipiendas approbatum,* secundum aliquos non requiritur, ut approbatus sit ab Ordinario loci, *in quo confessio fit,* sed sufficit, ut ab *aliquo* loci Ordinario iurisdictionem in mulieres receperit, atque etiam nunc ea fruatur. Haec tamen sententia, quamvis littera ei suffragetur, non videtur admittenda, nimirum, spectata indole totius legislationis, quae continuo requirit iurisdictionem collatum ab Ordinario loci, *in quo instituitur confessio.*"

[85] *Theologia Moralis,* II, n. 377.

possesses the same jurisdiction from the local ordinary as the confessor in canon 522.[86]

While admitting the general principle that confessional jurisdiction flows from the ordinary of the place in which the confessions are heard, one may nevertheless rightfully contend that in the subject under discussion emphasis should be placed on canon 876 rather than on canon 874. It is the former canon rather than the latter which legislates particularly for the confessor of nuns. Canon 876, § § 1 and 2, while stating that special jurisdiction is necessary in order that priests may hear the confessions of women religious and novices, and that this special jurisdiction is conferred by the ordinary of the place in which the house of these religious is located, nevertheless explicitly makes three exceptions to this principle.[87]

In these three exceptions the law as stated in canon 876 obviously does not have place. In order to discover what law does govern in such cases, recourse must be had to the exceptions themselves, and their meaning must be judged in the light of canon 18.[88]

The three exceptions to the general principle stated in canon 876 are canons 239, § 1, n. 1, 522, and 523. The first of these, canon 239, § 1, n. 1, grants to cardinals the privilege of hearing confessions, even the confessions of religious of either sex, anywhere in the world; jurisdiction from the local ordinary is not necessary for the simple reason that the canon does not demand it. The second, canon 522, speaks

---

[86] Cf. Mahoney, *Questions and Answers, The Sacraments* (London: Burns Oates & Washbourne, 1947), q. 203, p. 232 (hereafter cited *The Sacraments*).

[87] Canon 876, § 1: Revocata qualibet contraria particulari lege seu privilegio, sacerdotes tum saeculares tum religiosi, cuiusvis gradus aut officii, ad confessiones quarumcumque religiosarum ac novitiarum valide et licite recipiendas peculiari iurisdictione indigent, salvo praescripto can. 239, § 1, n. 1, 522, 523.

§ 2. Hanc iurisdictionem confert loci Ordinarius, ubi religiosarum domus sita est, ad normam can. 525.

[88] Canon 18: Leges ecclesiasticae intelligendae sunt secundum propriam verborum significationem in textu et contextu consideratam; quae si dubia et obscura manserit, ad locos Codicis parallelos, si qui sint, ad legis finem ac circumstantias et ad mentem legislatoris est recurrendum.

of the occasional confessor for any woman religious; here the jurisdiction of the ordinary of the place is necessary for the simple reason that the canon explicitly states that such a religious may approach *a confessor approved for women by the local ordinary.* The third, canon 523, treats of the occasional confessor for a woman religious who is gravely ill; it is logical to conclude that here the jurisdiction granted by the ordinary of the place is not necessary for the simple reason that jurisdiction from the ordinary of the place is not even mentioned, and the omission appears to be deliberate.

The point may be raised that a literal interpretation of the phrase "*approved to hear the confessions of women,*" as contained in canon 523, could lead to the conclusion that a Regular approved by a competent religious superior would thus likewise be included under this canon. Such an objection has no value for the reason that a religious superior cannot grant jurisdiction for the act of hearing the confessions of women; the legislation of the Code restricts his competence, in general, to those who are subject to him either by reason of the vow or by reason of service.[89]

Likewise the decision of the Code Commission to the effect that the term "*Ordinary*" as mentioned in connection with the maritime faculties of canon 883, § 1, does not include the major superior of an exempt clerical institute[90] does not militate against the argument offered above. Such a major superior, according to the principles of the Code, cannot grant faculties for the purpose of hearing the confessions of the faithful in general; his jurisdiction extends only to his own subjects and to those who live in the religious house day and night as servants, guests, students, or for the sake of their health.[91]

The second opinion, therefore, which deems jurisdiction from *any* local ordinary sufficient for the valid and licit application and use of canon 523, seems to be the one more favored by the wording of the text of the canon itself, and hence the one in accord with the mind of the legislator.

---

[89] Cf. canons 875, § 1, and 514, § 1.

[90] 30 iul. 1934—Bouscaren, *The Canon Law Digest,* II, p. 218.

[91] Cf. canons 875, § 1, and 514, § 1.

The problem, of course, is by no means definitively solved. But the very least that can be said is that a *dubium iuris* exists.[92] If a confessor who is approved by *some* local ordinary should hear the confession of a woman religious, whether nun, sister, or novice, who is gravely ill, the application of canon 209[93] renders his jurisdiction certain in the act of granting absolution.

Any Regular confessor, therefore, who has jurisdiction for the confessions of women from *any* local ordinary, and who is summoned or requested by a seriously sick nun, sister, or novice, anywhere in the world, in any diocese at all, to hear her confession, need not have any scruples in doing so, because such a confession is certainly both valid and licit in virtue of canons 523 and 209.

---

[92] Cf. Mahoney, *The Sacraments*, q. 203, p. 233.

[93] ... in dubio positivo et probabili sive iuris sive facti, iurisdictionem supplet Ecclesia pro foro tum externo tum interno.

CHAPTER III

PRIVILEGE OF THE ITINERANT REGULAR

Confessional jurisdiction, according to canon 874, § 1, is conferred upon priests by the ordinary of the place in which the confessions are heard. While this is the general law, the canon contains no clause that abrogates any privilege which may exempt a person, whether physical or moral, from its obligation.[1]

Capobianco, a Franciscan canonist, mentions the existence of such a privilege.[2] He claims that Franciscan confessors who are approved by the ordinary of some diocese can probably, while they are on a journey and are unable to approach the local ordinary, hear the confessions of the faithful and absolve them. The source of their privilege is twofold: a direct grant and the agency of the intercommunication of privileges among religious Orders in the past.

At first glance the probability that such a privilege still exists seems far-fetched, particularly in view of the unequivocal language used by Urban VIII (1623-1644). In the year 1628 this pontiff reiterated the necessity of episcopal approbation for hearing the confessions of seculars, and abrogated any indult enjoyed by Regulars to the contrary.[3] Nevertheless, the privilege was still mentioned or discussed by authors up to the time immediately preceding the Code of Canon Law. Such a privilege is well worth examining in detail, for, if it does exist, it is enjoyed by all Regulars in virtue of the acknowledged intercommunication of privileges.

---

[1] "Codex ius commune stratuit. Potest autem quis regularis exemptus ad specialia privilegia alicui Ordini concessa adhuc appellare; privilegia enim hoc canone expresse non revocantur."—Coronata, *De Sacramentis*, I, 344, nota 1.

[2] *Privilegia*, n. 106.

[3] Const. *Cum sicut*, 12 sept. 1628—*Fontes*, n. 208; cf. *supra*, p. 26

Article 1. Historical Background

In the year 1446 Eugene IV (1431 - 1447) granted to all the confessors of the Order of Friars Minor the privilege of hearing confessions whenever, because of the fact that they were traveling, they could not conveniently present themselves to the bishops and obtain faculties.[4] Sixtus IV (1471 - 1484) granted practically the same favor to the Friars Minor in the year 1476.[5]

A similar privilege was granted to the Jesuits in the year 1574 by Gregory XIII (1572 - 1585). The confessors of the Society of Jesus who had once been approved by an ordinary and who were appointed for the duty of hearing confessions by their own superiors were empowered, whenever they made a journey on land or sea, to hear the confessions of any of the faithful, provided that they did not perform this ministry against the will of the pastors of churches or in towns or places where there were ordinaries; in the places in which there were ordinaries, the permission of these had to be obtained.[6]

Such were the privileges granted to the Franciscans and to the Jesuits. It now remains to discover the views of the authors concerning

[4] Vivae vocis oraculum: "Quod quando non possunt commode se praesentare episcopis quia sunt in itinere vel alibi, et non possunt petere casus episcopales, eo casu possunt plenarie uti auctoritate episcopali."—Augustinus, p. 139, n. 24.

[5] Vivae vocis oraculum: "Idem [i.e., Sixtus IV] iisdem [i. e., Minoribus] concessit quod confessores dum sunt in itinere et requiruntur, possint audire confessiones sicut parochiani, etsi non fuerint praesentati secundum formam Clementinas."—Augustinus, p. 147, n. 42.

[6] "Concessit quod confessarii Societatis Iesu ac praedicatores ab aliquo ordinario semel approbati, et a suis superioribus ad huiusmodi munera deputati quandocunque sive in mari sive in terra iter faciant, possunt, non repugnantibus tamen curatis parochialium, Ecclesiarum, verbum Dei praedicare, et quorumcumque Christi fidelium confessiones audire, dummodo. id non faciant in oppidis aut locis, in quibus ordinarii existunt, nisi eorum licentia desuper obtenta."—Rodriguez, *Quaestiones Regulares et Canonicae*, t. I, q. 59 art. 5. This constitution of Gregory XIII is entitled *Decet Romanum Pontificem*, and is to be found in the *Institutum Societatis Ieus*, I, 56—cf. Capobianco, *Privilegia*, p. 128, nota 2; Augustinus, p. 158. n. 69.

them in the years that followed. Suarez (1548 - 1617)[7] and Lugo (1583 - 1660)[8] both mentioned the privilege of Gregory XIII. Lugo stated that the Jesuits *had* such a privilege and that it did not seem to be the one of which Urban VIII spoke in his decree of 1628.[9]

Diana (1585 - 1663) asserted that a Regular confessor who had been approved by the bishop of one diocese could hear confessions in another when he was on a journey, provided that he could not conveniently present himself to the bishop, and that the pastors were not opposed to it. He cited Eugene IV and Gregory XIII as the sources of this privilege, but added that there was a doubt whether it had been revoked by the constitution of Urban VIII, enacted in 1628.[10]

Reiffenstuel (1642 - 1703) made a similar statement, adding that the privilege of Gregory XIII made an exception with regard to those places in which the bishop was personally available.[11] After quoting a number of authors in support of the view that the privilege still existed in his day, he went on to say that even if it did not exist, Regulars in Germany could hear confessions under the same conditions because of the tacit consent of the bishop.[12]

Didacus of Aragon (+1763) denied that Regulars, once they were approved, could hear confessions in those places through which they passed, even if there were no ordinaries in such places and the pastors were not opposed to it. In accordance with the decree of the Council of Trent, Regulars needed to have the permission of the ordinary of the place where they were. As far as he was concerned, the privilege of Gregory XIII was revoked by the constitutions of Urban VIII and Clement X.[13]

---

[7] *Opera Omnia,* XXII, disp. 27, sect. 6, n. 13.

[8] *Opera Omnia* (8 vols. in 5, Venetiis, 1751), VI, disp. 21, sect. 2, n. 29.

[9] *Loc. cit.*

[10] Cotinio, *Summa Diana* (Venetiis, 1668), s. v. "Confessarius Regularis," n. 9.

[11] *Ius Canonicum Universum,* lib. V, tit. 39, n. 259.

[12] *Loc. cit.*

[13] Didacus ab Aragonia, *Dilucidatio Privilegiorum Ordinum Regularium, praesertim Mendicantium* (Bononiae, 1753), tr. VI, cap. III, n. 22.

Thenhaven, who flourished about the year 1739, maintained that, in virtue of the privilege of Gregory XIII, the Jesuits and Mendicants, when they had been approved by one bishop, could, while they were on a journey, hear the confessions of seculars anywhere, except in those places in which the permission of the ordinary could easily be obtained. According to him, the opinion which contended that the privilege was not revoked by Clement X stood truly probable; if, however, it was false, then the Church supplied whatever jurisdiction was wanting.[14]

The existence of the privilege was mentioned by Elbel (1690-1756), and apparently acknowledged by Bierbaum (1843-1907), who brought the work of the former up to date.[15] These two moralists, whose treatise on moral theology was based on the case system, presented and solved two significant cases.

The first case dealt with a religious who was sent from a convent in one diocese to a convent in another, in which new place he had never received episcopal approbation. Soon after his arrival, his superior presented him to the local ordinary for the examination. In the meantime the throng of penitents at the convent was so great that the other confessors of the same convent did not seem sufficient to take care of them. The new religious, therefore, was ordered to hear confessions. Could this religious obey the command lawfully?[16]

Towards the end of the solution of this case, there was raised the question whether or not a religious, although not approved in the diocese, but on a journey, could licitly accede to the request of a pastor to hear his confession or to render him aid in hearing the confessions of his parishioners. The authors answered that he could probably do so licitly. In support of their answer they cited a number of authors who based their opinion both on the tacit consent of the ordinary and on the privilege granted by Eugene IV and by Gregory XIII under the

---

[14] *Nucleus Theologiae Canonico-Moralis* (Coesfeldiae, 1726), p. 411.

[15] Elbel-Bierbaum, *Theologia Moralis* (3. ed., 3 vols., Paderbonae, 1904-1907).

[16] Elbel-Bierbaum, *op. cit.*, III, pars IX, conferentia XI, n. 288ss.

following conditions: 1) that the confessor be approved by at least one bishop; 2) that he do not hear confessions in the place where the bishop was present; 3) that he do not hear confessions when the pastor was opposed to it; and 4) that he do not hear confessions where he as a religious was going to dwell habitually.[17] It was the opinion of these writers that since many authors regarded the privilege as revoked by the constitution of Clement X, it should no longer be used in the absence of any and every necessity or urgent cause.[18]

The second case was concerned with a religious who went from one diocese, together with some friends, to honor a shrine of the Blessed Virgin in another diocese. While there he was asked by his traveling companions to hear their confessions. The religious refused on the ground that he had never been approved in this particular diocese. When he noted, however, that his friends felt badly about it, he yielded to their entreaties, hear their confessions and absolved them in a private room. Did he do well?[19]

The authors answered that the religious did not act well, and for this reason: according to the Constitution *Superna* of Clement X, Regulars who were approved in one diocese were not thereby to be considered as approved everywhere; consequently, they could not licitly hear confessions in a strange diocese without the approbation of the ordinary.[20] The authors went on to state, however,—and this concerned the point at issue—that even though the religious could probably have absolved validly in virtue of the privilege granted by Gregory XIII to those on a journey, nevertheless this privilege was never to be used in the absence of a grave cause.[21]

In the two cases here discussed, the Regular confessor *probably* absolved validly in virtue of the privilege under discussion.

---

[17] *Ibid.*, n. 290.

[18] *Loc. cit.*

[19] Elbel-Bierbaum, *op. cit.*, III, pars IX, conferentia XII, n. 317ss.

[20] *Ibid.*, n. 317.

[21] *Loc. cit.*

Article 2. Interpretation of the Facts

So much for the facts of history. These facts reveal that prior to the promulgation of the Code of Canon Law there existed a probable opinion that Regular confessors, in virtue of a papal privilege, could absolve penitents in any diocese through which they journeyed, provided they had been approved by the ordinary of some diocese and were unable to approach the ordinary of the territory in which they were, and provided also that they did not hear confessions when the pastor was opposed to it.

There now arises the question whether the same probability exists under the Code. The answer to this question can be discovered only through a study of canon 4 of the Code of Canon Law, for this canon implements the means and delineates the factors in accordance with which privileges that obtained in the past still retain their efficacy for the present.

According to this canon, four conditions must be fulfilled if a pre-Code privilege is to retain its effect: 1) the privilege must have been granted by the Apostolic See to a physical or moral person; 2) the privilege must not have been revoked; 3) the privilege must still have been in use at the time of the promulgation of the Code; and 4) the privilege must not have been expressly revoked in any of the canons of the Code. [22]

The *first* of these conditions has certainly been verified, as the history of this privilege of the itinerant Regular has clearly shown.

The *third* condition has likewise been fulfilled. A privilege is the grant of a special right made by a legitimate superior. [23] It is a favorable privilege if it does not injure the rights of a third person; otherwise it is odious. [24] If the privilege exempts a person or a thing from

---

[22] Cf. canon 4; Shuhler, *Privileges of Regulars,* p. 33.

[23] Roelker, *Principles of Privilege according to the Code of Canon Law,* The Catholic University of America Canon Law Studies, n. 35 (Washington, D.C.: The Catholic University of America, 1926), p. 16.

[24] Roelker, *op. cit.,* p. 33.

the law, it is termed a privilege contrary to the law; if, on the other hand, it does no violence to an enacted law, if it is something that is neither prohibited nor permitted by the law, it is called a privilege beyond the law.[25]

The privilege of the itinerant Regular confessor is certainly of a favorable and not of an offensive or obtrusive character, since it does not violate the right of any third person; the right of the local ordinary in canon 874, § 1, remains intact. And since canon 874, § 1, neither permits nor prohibits the privilege under discussion, the privilege must be termed a privilege beyond the law. Its non-use does not effect cr connote its revocation.[26] Hence the *third* condition as above stated seems reasonably verified.

The *fourth* condition has likewise been fulfilled, since canon 874 contains no clause that abrogates existing privileges.[27]

The only condition that needs to be verified is the *second*, namely, that which demands that the privilege must never have been revoked.

Those who assert the revocation of this privilege appeal to the constitutions of Urban VIII (1623-1644) and Clement X (1670-1676). The former pope, in his Constitution *Cum sicut*,[28] abrogated any and every indult possessed by Regulars in virtue of which they were exempted from the necessity of receiving episcopal approbation for the act of hearing the confessions of seculars. Clement X, in his Constitution *Superna*,[29] reiterated the need for episcopal approbation from the ordinary of the diocese in which the confessions were to be heard.

It seems that these two papal documents were directed against an abuse. They were directed against those Regulars who considered

---

[25] Roelker, *op. cit.*, p. 31; Capobianco, *Privilegia*, n. 2.

[26] According to canon 76, a privilege that does not injure the right of a third party does not cease through non-use.

[27] Cf. *supra*, p. 70, note 1.

[28] 12 sept. 1628—*Fontes*, n. 208; *supra*, p. 26.

[29] 21 iul. 1670—*Fontes*, n. 246; *supra*, p. 26.

approbation received from one ordinary sufficient to enable them to hear confessions in the diocese of any ordinary where they stayed *habitually.* It seems reasonable to conclude that these pontiffs had neither in mind nor in intention the case of the Regular who was *on a journey.*[30] Hence the privilege granted to the itinerant Regular confessor was *probably* never revoked. The *second* condition set in canon 4 seems then likewise to be fulfilled, and it seems safe to conclude that the existence of the privilege in the present law has solid probabiliy in is favor.

ARTICLE 3. THE MEANING OF THE PRIVILEGE

The modern canonists who refer explicitly to this privilege are Capobianco,[31] Coronata[32] and O'Brien.[33] Yet there is a difference in their interpretation of it. Capobianco asserts that the privilege can be used anywhere, provided that the local ordinary cannot be approached conveniently for faculties.[34] Coronata seems to restrict its practical value to pagan countries.[35] O'Brien agrees with Coronata.[36] The problem, therefore, of the meaning of the privilege granted to the itinerant Regular confessor must be discussed.

According to Eugene IV (1431 - 1447), those friars confessors who were on a journey and could not conveniently present themselves to the bishop for faculties could hear confessions.[37] The wording of the privilege granted by Gregory XIII (1572 - 1585) to the Jesuirs is slightly different. This pontiff reigned after the Council of Trent (1545 - 1563); he, therefore, insisted on the necessity of receiving

[30] Cf. Reiffenstuel, *Ius Canonicum Universum,* lib. V, tit. 39, n. 259.

[31] *Privilegia,* n. 106.

[32] *Institutiones,* I, 820.

[33] *The Exemption of Religious in Church Law,* p. 177.

[34] *Loc. cit.*

[35] Coronata, *ibid.,* nota 2.

[36] O'Brien, *loc. cit.*

[37] Cf. Augustinus, p. 139, n. 24; *supra,* p. 71.

approbation from some local ordinary. The use of the privilege granted by Gregory XIII was restricted in two instances: 1) if the pastors objected to its use; and 2) if the ordinary was present in the place where the use of the privilege might be invoked.

With regard to this latter restriction, the pope used the words *in oppidis aut locis.* [38] The pontiff apparently did not intend to restrict the use of the privilege to those territories over which no bishop ruled. His intention, on the contrary, was to restrict its use in the case in which a bishop or local ordinary was actually present in a particular place; for in such cases the Jesuit confessor, even though on a journey, would have no trouble in approaching the ordinary for faculties.

With reference to the first restriction, Pope Gregory used the words *curatis parochialium Ecclesiarium* in stating that the privilege could not be used if the pastors of parochial churches objected. [39] Now, the terms "pastors and parochial churches" refer to a definite territorial organization subject to an ordinary.

This interpretation seems to be borne out by Reiffenstuel, [40] who, when he referred to the instances in which the privilege could not be used, spoke of the bishop as being present *personaliter.* This interpretation seems likewise a reasonable explanation of the grant when one views the expressions used by some pre-Code authors, expressions such as "those places excepted in which the permission of the ordinary can be obtained conveniently."[41] The interpretation is further supported by a review of the two cases given by Elbel-Bierbaum.[42]

O'Brien, in his interpretation, follows Coronata. Both of these apparently depend upon Piat (1815-1904). The latter [43] listed the au-

---

[38] Cf. *supra,* p. 71, note 6.

[39] Cf. *supra,* p. 71, note 6.

[40] *Ius Canonicum Universum,* lib. 5, tit. 39, n. 259.

[41] "...exceptis locis, in quibus licentia Ordinarii commode obtinibilis." —Thenhaven, *Nucleus Theologiae Canonico-Moralis,* p. 411; cf. *supra,* p. 73.

[42] *Theologia Moralis,* III, pars IX, conferentiae XI et XII, nn. 288ss et 317ss; cf. *supra,* pp. 73-74.

[43] *Praelectiones Iuris Regularis* (3. ed., 2 vols., Tornaci: Casterman, 1906), II, Q. 236, p. 195.

thors who upheld the continued existence of the privilege, together with those who denied its continued existence. He asserted that the common opinion denied the continued existence of the privilege. That is why Coronata, in a footnote,[44] states that Piat seemed to deny the privilege, adding that, in his own view, the privilege seems to be of value in infidel countries.

While Coronata and O'Brien admit in substance the existence of the privilege of the itinerant Regular confessor, they have apparently misinterpreted it by limiting its use to places where there are no local ordinaries. Rather, the conclusion that the privilege remains applicable as long as a local ordinary cannot readily be sought for faculties seems to be the one that is justified from the discussion contained in the present chapter. So the view of Capobianco[45] appears to approach the correct opinion more closely than does that maintained by Coronata and O'Brien: this privilege can be used, provided that the local ordinary cannot be conveniently approached for faculties.

In conclusion, then, it may be stated with sufficient probability that a Regular confessor, once he has obtained and still retains jurisdiction from some local ordinary, may while on a journey and unable to approach the ordinary of the place conveniently for faculties, validly hear the confessions of the faithful if the pastor is not apposed to it.[46]

The Regular confessor has no need of a cause or of a necessity to render his action lawful. In this particular instance there is question of a positive and probable doubt of law concerning the possession of jurisdiction. In such a doubt there is no necessity for the existence of some cause or reason in order to impart absolution validly and licitly.[47]

---

[44] *Institutiones,* I, 820, nota 2.

[45] *Privilegia,* n. 106.

[46] Capobianco (*loc. cit.*) makes no mention of the lack of opposition of the pastor. Since this lack of opposition is set forth in the privilege granted by Gregory XIII as a condition, it seems safer to insist upon it in discussing the privilege.

[47] Cappello, *De Sacramentis,* II, n. 347.

CHAPTER IV

EXTRAORDINARY FACULTIES

ARTICAL 1. INTRODUCTION

The content of the diocesan faculties of the Regular confessor depends upon the powers granted to him by the local ordinary. Once, however, the Regular has obtained jurisdiction over the faithful, the preliminary requisite is fulfilled for the use of the faculties he enjoys in virtue of apostolic privileges.

While the present chapter is concerned only with the privilege of absolving from those automatic censures which are reserved by the general law to the local ordinary, it must not be forgotten that Regulars enjoy other extraordinary faculties which they can exercise when they have obtained jurisdiction from the local ordinary. These faculties should be mentioned, at least in passing.

Regular confessors have the privilege both of dispensing the faithful from private vows and of commuting such vows in the internal forum, whether sacramental or extra-sacramental, so long as these vows are not reserved and the rights of a third party are not injured by the use of this privilege. [1] They likewise possess the privilege of dispensing from irregularities which result from an occult delict, [2] unless these irregularities are connected with cases of voluntary homicide, or the

[1] Shuhler, *Privileges of Regulars*, pp. 133, 136, 170.

[2] A delict is occult when it has not as yet been divulged and when, in view of the circumstances under which it was committed, one can prudently judge that it will not easily be divulged. Cf. canon 2197, 1° and 4°; Vermeersch-Creusen, *Epitome Iuris Canonici* (6. ed., 3 vols., Mechlinae-Romae: Dessain, 1937-1946), II, 261 (hereafter cited *Epitome*).

effective procurement of an abortion, or with cases that have been brought to a court.[3] This dispensation, which the Regular can grant only in the internal sacramental forum, i.e., in the act of hearing sacramental confessions, may be used with a view to allowing the penitent both to receive Holy Orders and to exercise those which he has already received.[4]

The historical portion of this dissertation was concerned, to a large extent, with the confessional privileges granted to Regulars by the various popes. As is evident from the historical summary,[5] these confessors, prior to the promulgation of the Code of Canon Law, enjoyed the privilege of absolving their penitents from censures reserved to the local ordinaries by the general law. The conditions set forth in canon 4[6] of the present Code for the effective transfer of pre-Code privileges into the Code itself have been verified in the case of this privilege of Regulars, a conclusion that has been borne out by a study of its relation to that particular canon.[7]

This conclusion receives further support from the weight of authority. Among the post-Code authors who maintain that Regular confessors enjoy this privilege under the Code of Canon Law can be

---

[3] A case is not considered as having been "brought to a judicial court" unless either a citation has been issued by the legitimate authority or the parties have appeared before the judge of their own free will; the denunciation of the guilty party does not in itself suffice. Cf. Vermeersch-Creusen, *loc. cit.*

[4] Shuhler, *op. cit.*, pp. 167-168, 170. Huser's statement to the effect that certain clerical exempt religious who enjoy the privileges of regulars can exercise special faculties, as listed by the authors, to dispense from the irregularity for abortion is open to misinterpretation—cf. Huser, *The Crime of Abortion in Canon Law*, The Catholic University of America Canon Law Studies, n. 162 (Washington, D. C.: The Catholic University of America Press, 1942), p. 133. His statement refers to religious who are ordinaries, or to those religious who as priests possess the privileges of Regulars and who are at the moment giving a mission or a retreat or some such public exercise. Cf. Vermeersch-Creusen, *Epitome*, II, n. 261.

[5] Cf. *supra*, p. 42.

[6] Cf. *supra*, p. 75.

[7] Cf. Shuhler, *Privileges of Regulars*, pp. 33, 95-99.

cited Pruemmer (1866-1931),[8] Fanfani,[9] Ubach (1871-1935),[10] Merkelbach (1871-1942),[11] Browne,[12] Genicot (1856-1900) - Salsmans (1873-1944),[13] Iorio,[14] Jone,[15] Bonzelet,[16] Gerster a Zeil,[17] Wouters (1864-1933),[18] Shuhler,[19] Capobianco,[20] Noldin (1838-1922) - Schmitt,[21] Aertnys (1828-1915) - Damen,[22] Claeys Bouua-

[8] *Manuale Iuris Ecclesiastici* (2. ed., Friburgi Brisgoviae: Herder, 1920), p. 314.

[9] *De Iure Religiosorum* (2. ed., Taurini-Romae: Marietti, 1925), n. 365.

[10] *Theologia Moralis* (2. ed., 2 vols., Bonis Auris: apud "Sociedad San Miguel", 1935), I, n. 1343: "Absolvere [tum Mendicantes tum ceteri regulares qui cum iisdem communicarunt] possunt *saeculares* a casibus Episcopo reservatis a iure ..."

[11] *Summa Theologia Moralis* (3. ed., vols., Parisiis: Desclée de Brouwer. 1938-1939), III, n. 598-B: "Confessarii regulares mendicantes, et qui participant mendicantium privilegia, a casibus *Ordinario,* non quidem auctoritate propria sed *de iure reservatis,* absolvere possunt ut v.g. a procuratione abortus."

[12] *Handbook of Notes on Theology,* p. 39.

[13] *Institutiones Theologiae Moralis* (11. ed. [4. ed. post Codicem Iuris Canonici], 2 vols., Bruxellis: Dewit, 1927), II, n. 604, nota (1):"...Iuxta sententiam quam S. Alphonsus tamquam probabiliorem sequitur, ab iis [i. e., censuris episcopis aliisque ordinariis reservatis a iure] absolvere possunt Regulares saltem Mendicantes: hoc enim privilegium nunquam revocatum est."

[14] *Compendium Theologiae Moralis* (5. ed., 2 vols., Neapoli: D'Auria, 1934-1935), II, n. 960, nota 3: "Iuxta S. Alf. 1. 7, 99, *regulares* saltem mendicantes ex privilegio apostolico (a Codice non revocato), absolvere possunt ab his [i.e., Ordinario reservatis *a iure*] censuris."

[15] *Moral Theology* (2. Eng. ed., tr. by Rev. Urban Adelman, Westminster, Md.: Newman, 1946), n. 416-2c.

[16] *The Pastoral Companion,* n. 257.

[17] *Ius Religiosorum in compendium redactum* (Taurini: Marietti, 1935), pp. 284-285.

[18] *Manuale Theologiae Moralis,* II, n. 865, nota 1.

[19] *Privileges of Regulars,* pp. 95-99.

[20] *Privilegia,* n. 117.

[21] *Summa Theologiae Moralis* (3 vols.: Vols. I-II, 27. ed., 1940-1941; Vol. III, 26. ed., 1940, Oeniponte: Rauch), III, n. 367.

[22] *Theologia Moralis,* II, n. 1067.

ert-Simenon,[23] Coronata,[24] Schaefer,[25] Beste,[26] and Vermeersch (1858-1936) - Creusen.[27]

Among the authors here cited, Geniot - Salsmans, Iorio, Ubach, and Merkelbach have been quoted *verbatim* in this article, for the reason that they seem either to imply that only the Mendicant Regulars possess this faculty,[28] or that the privilege is the common property of the Mendicants and *only* those other Regulars who have *specifically* received the right to share in the privileges of the Mendicants.[29] The other authors named in support of the existence of the privilege under the legislation of the Code do not mention any such restrictions. And no such restriction is warranted. Even before the Code it was the common opinion, according to Mocchegiani (1839-1905),[30] that the intercommunication of privileges existed between the Mendicant Orders and any and all of the other non-Mendicant Orders.

A Regular confessor need have no fear or scruple in using the faculty to absolve penitents from any censure that is at one and the same time automatically incurred and reserved by the general law to the local ordinary.

Certain points concerning the exercise of this privilege need clarification.

First of all, it is not at all necessary that Regular confessors possess confessional jurisdiction in their respective Orders before they can enjoy the right to exercise this extraordinary faculty. All that is necessary is that they have diocesan jurisdiction and that they exercise this

---

[23] *Manuale Iuris Canonici* (3 vols.: Vol. I, 4. ed., 1934; Vol. II, 2. ed., 1935; Vol. III, 3. ed., 1931, Gandae et Leodii: apud auctores, 1931-1935), I, n. 680.

[24] *Institutiones,* I, 819.

[25] *De Religiosis,* n. 446 c.

[26] *Introductio,* p. 498, nota 3.

[27] *Epitome,* I, n. 785.

[28] Genicot-Salsmans and Iorio, *supra,* notes 13 and 14 respectively.

[29] Ubach and Merkelbach, *supra,* notes 10 and 11 respectively.

[30] *Iurisprudentia Ecclesiastica,* I, n. 681; cf. Introduction, *supra,* p. 7.

with at least the presumed permision of their superiors. Capobianco [31] seems to place undue stress on the necessity of jurisdiction delegated by the competent superior before the religious priests can be termed "Regular confessors" and obtain the privileges of Regular confessors. However, he seems to soften this somewhat by stating that the privileges of Regular confessors are communicated by means of the jurisdiction, *or the permission,* [32] received from the proper competent prelate of the Order. [33]

It sometimes happens that Regular priests who have not received delegated jurisdiction from their competent superiors to hear the confessions of the subjects of the religious province or Order are nevertheless presented to the local ordinary for faculties to hear the confessions of the faithful in the diocese. This procedure does not of itself deprive the Regulars of the use of the privilege to absolve their penitents from the automatic censures reserved by the general law to the local ordinary.

Such seems the logical conclusion to be deduced from a study of the history of this papal grant. At the particular period in history when the sovereign pontiffs bestowed upon Regulars the authority and power to absolve from censures, religious themselves were bound by a strict law to confess their sins to their superiors or to priests appointed by their superiors. This historical fact makes it seem likely that many of the Regular confessors in those days were confessors of secular penitents and not confessors of religious. In other words, they did not necessarily have jurisdiction in their own Orders in view of the fact that they heard the confessions of the faithful.

It seems to follow that the majority of Regular confessors were appointed by their superiors to the office of hearing the confessions of the faithful alone. In virtue of this appointment they received from their superiors, who acted as delegates of the Holy See in this matter, the faculty to absolve from censures.

---

[31] *Privilegia,* nn. 95-96.

[32] Italics are those of the present author.

[33] *Ibid.,* n. 96.

Hence under the present legislation of the Code, the grant of episcopal jurisdiction being postulated as present, the permission of the competent superior—whether that permission be express, tacit, or presumed—suffices for the valid and licit exercise of this power. Only when the superior expressly states that he is not granting the privilege, or when he is opposed to the confessor's exercise of jurisdiction, [34] does the latter cease to be a *Regular confessor* in the technical sense; in this hypothesis the confessor is unable to make use of the extraordinary faculties that are granted by the Holy See, for the reason that these powers were granted, not to the confessors individually but directly to the Order and the superiors, and only through these to the confessor.

Closely connected with this point there is another that should be clarified. According to the language employed by some authors, the privilege under discussion embraces censures reserved by the general law to the *bishop;* [35] other authors use the term *ordinary.* [36] The use of such terminology is justified, provided it is properly understood. In ordinary language these terms are often interchanged. It should be noted, however, that in strict legal terminology the words "bishop" and "ordinary" are by no means synonymous. [37] To restrict the use of the privilege to the absolution from censures reserved to the *bishop* alone is just as unwarranted as to extend it to the absolution from those reserved to *any ordinary* at all.

The privilege under discussion seems to have been granted originally to Regular confessors for the benefit of the *faithful.* From the viewpoint of the penitential dicipline, the religious of those days were strictly bound within, and subject to, the regulations of their own particular

---

[34] A competent superior's opposition, of course, is of no avail with reference to the jurisdiction exercised in the circumstances envisioned in canon 519.

[35] Pruemmer, *Manuale Iuris Ecclesiastici,* p. 314; Vermeersch-Creusen, *Epitome,* I, n. 785.

[36] Schaefer, *De Religiosis,* n. 446 c; Shuhler, *Privileges of Regulars,* pp. 97-99.

[37] Cf. canon 198, §§ 1 and 2.

legislation, especially in regard to the choice of confessors. Consequently, it seems that they were incapable of enjoying the benefit of the absolution from these automatic censures imparted by Regular confessors in virtue of papal privileges.

The purpose of the foregoing observations is merely to point out that Regulars apparently received no power in virtue of the privilege under discussion to absolve religious subjects from the automatic censures, if any, that were reserved by the general law to their own *religious ordinary*. This does not mean that Regular confessors cannot absolve religious from the automatic censures reserved by the general law to the *local ordinary*. The contrary is true.

The practical application of the foregoing distinction is apparent. Whenever one of these censures is reserved to the *ordinary*, then a local ordinary, with reference to his own subjects and to strangers in the territory, and a religious ordinary, with reference to his own subjects, can impart absolution;[38] the Regular confessor can grant absolution from these censures wherever the local ordinary can. Therefore, in the case in which the censure is reserved to the *proper* ordinary,[39] a distinction must be made. If the proper ordinary is the local ordinary, the Regular confessor may use his faculty; if, on the contrary, the proper ordinary is the major superior of a religious institute, it seems that the Regular confessor has no power in virtue of the papal privilege.

In view of what has been stated, it seems more precise to state that Regular confessors can absolve penitents from censures reserved by the general law to the ordinary in all cases in which that ordinary is the local ordinary. According to the Code of Canon Law the local ordinary includes the Roman Pontiff, residential bishops, abbots and prelates *nullius* (including the vicars general of the foregoing), diocesan administrators, vicars and prefects apostolic, and all those who succeed to their position by law, or in accordance with approved constitutions, when they are not in power or cannot exercise it; the major superior in an exempt clerical institute is not a local ordinary.[40]

---

[38] Cf. canon 2253, 3°.

[39] As in canon 2343, § 4.

[40] Cf. canon 198, §§ 1 and 2.

A third point which needs some clarification concerns the forum in which the Regular confessor can excercise this privilege. The power of jurisdiction can exist for either the external or the internal forum; the latter, called also the forum of conscience. can be either sacramental or extra-sacramental.[41] Clement X (1670-1676) stated definitely that Regulars could not in virtue of their privileges absolve penitents from censures in the external forum. The language used by the pontiff seems to imply that Regulars could not use their privilege in the internal *extra-sacramental* forum either, for he went on to say that penitents absolved in the *penitential* forum were not considered absolved in the external forum,, and, consequently, could be forced by bishops to conduct themselves as still under censure, even though they had been absolved by Regulars.[42]

Inasmuch as the pope referred to the use of the privilege in the *penitential* forum, thereby excluding the possibility of its use in the extra-sacramental internal forum, the privilege appears to have been restricted in its use to the internal *sacramental* forum. The statement used by some authors, such as Aertnys-Damen,[43] Pruemmer,[44] and Schaefer,[45] to the effect that Regulars can absolve from these censures in the form of conscience is misleading. It seems more correct to state that this privilege can be used only in the internal sacramental forum[46] And, in passing, stress must be placed upon the fact that the Regular confessor can exercise this faculty not only in occult cases, but likewise in those that are public.[47] The question of prudence in this re-

---

[41] Canon 196.

[42] Const. *Superna,* 21 iun. 1670, § 7—*Fontes,* n. 246; *supra,* p. 34.

[43] *Theologia Moralis,* II, n. 1067.

[44] *Manuale Iuris Ecclesiastici.* p. 314

[45] *De Religiosis,* n. 446 c.

[46] Cf. Vitall, "De reservationibus pontificiis a iure reservatis ordinario deque regularium privilegio ab iisdem absolvendi"—*CpR,* XIV (1933), 445, n. XIV; Shuhler, *Privileges of Regulars,* p. 169, n. 2.

[47] Cf. Vitali, *loc. cit.;* Shuhler, *op. cit.,* pp. 115-116. Regulars are advised not to use the privilege in cases wherein a public reparation or reconciliation is necessary, except in urgent necessity. Cf. Shuhler, *loc. cit.,* and Bonzelet, *The Pastoral Companion.* n. 257, where the attempted marriage of a Catholic before a non-Catholic minister is given as an example.

gard is another matter; at this point emphasis is placed only on the validity of the absolution.

In conclusion, then, it may be stated that Regular confessors, provided they have at least the presumed permission from their competent superior, and jurisdiction from the local ordinary, possess the power to absolve any penitent, secular or religious, in the internal sacramental forum from any automatic censure reserved by the general law to an ordinary who is a local ordinary. The remainder of this chapter is devoted to the enumeration and discussion of such penalties, preceded by a short treatment on the notion of censure.

Article 2 Preliminary Notions Concerning Censures

A censure, as defined by the Code of Canon Law, [48] is a penalty by which a baptized person, who has committed a delict and is contumacious or obstinate, is deprived of certain spiritual goods, or of goods connected with the spiritual, until he gives up his obstinacy and is absolved. This penalty, by its very nature, is medicinal, not vindictive, since its primary purpose is to prohibit the crime and to correct the erring ways of the sinner. [49] Hence it can only be inflicted upon, or incurred by, an offender who is contumacious. The censure can be removed by absolution alone, but once the guilty person has abandoned his obstinancy or contumacy, such absolution cannot be denied. [50]

The Code considers such a person to have abandoned his contumacy when he is truly sorry for the delict he has committed and at the same time has given, or seriously promises to give, fitting satisfaction for the damage and scandal he has caused. [51] The judgment whether or not the repentance is sincere, the satisfaction sufficient, or the promise serious, is to be made by the individual from whom the absolution is sought.

---

[48] Canon 2241, § 1.

[49] Cf. Cipollini, *De Censuris Latae Sententiae iuxta Codicem Iuris Canonici* (Taurini: Marietti 1925), n. 1 (hereafter cited *De Censuris*).

[50] Canon 2248, § 2.

[51] Canon 2242, § 3.

In the light of all this it follows that the Regular confessor will be the judge in the internal sacramental forum of the cases presented to him which involve any of the automatic censures reserved to the local ordinary by the general law. It likewise follows that just as a confessor may not refuse absolution to a penitent who is worthily disposed, so the Regular confessor may not *arbitrarily* refuse to exercise his privilege in favor of a penitent if the latter is properly disposed and the conditions necessary for absolution from a censure have been fulfilled. [52] The privilege has been granted to him, not for his own good, but for the welfare of the penitent. In accordance with this latter principle, of course, there are times when he may *prudently* refuse absolution and chose rather to follow the ordinary procedure. [53]

A censure is a serious punishment. Particularly is this true of those censures that are incurred automatically. It is in accordance not only with the spirit of the Code, but with its very language,[54] that a censure of any type should be inflicted only with great circumspection.

Like other penalties, censures are likewise subject to strict interpretation. [55] Unless the terminology of the penal law and sanction is literally fulfilled, the delict is not committed nor is the censure incurred. No matter how analogous or parallel cases may appear to be, no matter how guilty are the persons involved, a censure cannot be incurred unless that particular case and that particular person or persons fall under the exact wording of the law containing the penal sanction. [56]

Knowledge and deliberation, which are necessary for the commission of any sin, are likewise necessary for the commission of a delict. Consequently, ignorance plays a great part in determining whether or not a given penalty has been incurred. Affected ignorance, which is in reality a mere pretense of an excuse for sin, never excuses one from incurring an automatic penalty enacted by law. [57]

---

[52] Cf. canons 2248, § 2, and 2242, § 3.

[53] Cf. Shuhler, *Privileges of Regulars*, pp. 114-115.

[54] Cf. canon 2241, § 2.

[55] Canon 19.

[56] Cf. canons 2219, § 3 and 2231.

[57] Canon 2229, § 1.

The legislator has, however, made certain other concessions to human weakness in the matter of penalties. Sometimes the penal law contains terminology that demands full knowledge and complete deliberation on the part of the offender; in such cases—always abstracted, of course, from affected ignorance, which is never an excuse—anything at all that diminishes imputability in even the slightest degree excuses a person from incurring a censure.[58]

If the law does not contain such terminology, then *simple* ignorance—that, namely, which remains in spite of some effort, albeit insufficient, to determine the truth—does excuse one from incurring a censure. If the ignorance is due to the fact that the offender exercised no effort or scarcely any effort to discover the true state of affairs, then it is called *crass* or *supine* ignorance and does *not* excuse the guilty person from incurring the censure.[59]

Attention to the preceding few principles is absolutely necessary for any discussion of the penal laws contained in Book V of the Code. If they are kept in mind it should be easier for the Regular confessor to act safely and prudently in the exercise of his papal privilege relative to the automatic censures that are reserved by the general law to the local ordinary. The following articles deal with these penalties.

Article 3 Censures Reserved By The General Law To The Local Ordinary

The Code of Canon Law contains twelve such censures, each of which is here given a brief treatment. The Regular confessor has the power to absolve from these penalties, whether the case be public or

[58] Cf canon 2229, § 2.

[59] Cf. canon 2229, § 3, 1º. With reference to fear, it is necessary to note the reply given on December 30, 1937, by the Pontifical Commsision for the Authentic Interpretation of the Code. According to the tenor of this reply, grave fear excuses from penalties *latae sententiae* if the crime, although intrinsecally wrong and gravely culpable, does not tend to the contempt of the faith or of ecclesiatical authority nor to the public harm of souls according to canon 2229, § 3, 3º.—Bouscaren, *The Canon Law Digest*, II, 570-571.

occult. He must, of course, act prudently: he must judge whether the penitent has abandoned his obstinacy, as is required by canon 2242, § 3.[60]

1. Marriage before a non-Catholic minister

Catholics who contract marriage before a non-Catholic minister in violation of canon 1063, § 1, incur automatically an excommunication reserved to the ordinary.[61] This penalty will be discussed in the fourth and final article of the present chapter.

2. Education of children outside the Catholic Church

An excommunication reserved to the ordinary is incurred automatically by Catholics who enter marriage with the explicit or implicit understanding that all the children or some of them are to be educated outside the Catholic Church.[62]

Since the language of the canon is general, it binds two Catholics as well as a Catholic and a non-Catholic who enter marriage with such an agreement. The agreement is implicit in the case of a mixed marriage where the non-Catholic refuses to accept the condition of the Catholic education of the children and the Catholic party acquiesces in this refusal; it is likewise implicit if the Catholic party obliges himself or herself to do all that pleases the other party relative to the religious education of the children.[63] It is possible for the same implicit agreement to be present in the marriage of two Catholics.

The agreement between the spouses must, of course, be a serious one, and it must precede or at least accompany the celebration of a true marriage. Hence the penalty of the canon is not incurred if the pact is made and is then followed by a mere civil ceremony;[64] nor

---

[60] Cf. *supra*, p. 88.

[61] Canon 2319, § 1, 1°.

[62] Canon 2319, § 1, 2°.

[63] Cf. Cipollini, *De Censuris*, n. 71; Cappello, *De Censuris* (2. ed., Taurinorum Augustae: Marietti, 1925), n. 370.

[64] Cappello, *loc. cit.*

does the penalty apply if the agreement is made but the marriage does not take place. [65] Neither is the censure incurred if the pact is made after a true marriage has been contracted. [66] Finally, the penalty is not incurred if the pact is revolked before the true marriage takes place. The literal fulfullment of the canon demands that a real marriage be contracted with the pact in question.

A slight problem arises relative to those who have been married civilly or who have been living in concubinage without any marriage ceremony at all. If such a couple, seeking to have their marriage convalidated or their union regularized, contract a true marriage with the serious agreement concerning the non-Catholic education of the children *already* born, what about the censure? In the eyes of Cerato such a couple—or the Catholic party in the case of a mixed marriage—incurs the excommunication since it makes no difference whether the pact is concerned with children to be born or already born. [67] According to Cocchi, however, the agreement that forms the basis for incurring the penalty concerns the children *to be born* of the marriage. [68]

The view of Cocchi seems the better one, and this for two reasons. First of all, the wording of the canon easily lends itself to the interpretation that only the *children of the marriage* are meant. Secondly, the practice of the Church seems to support this opinion; a response of the Holy Office, given on January 16, 1942, [69] leaves no doubt that the *cautiones* in a mixed marriage do not of themselves include the children born before the marriage.

---

[65] Sipos, *Enchiridion Iuris Canonici* (3. ed.,, Pecs: Ex Typographia "Haladas R. T.", 1936), p. 553.

[66] Chelodi, *Ius Poenale et Ordo Procedendi in iudiciis criminalibus iuxta Codicem Iuris Canonici* (4. ed., Tridenti: Libreria Moderna Editrice A. Ardesi, 1935), n. 60, ad 5 (hereafter cited *Ius Poenale*).

[67] *Censurae vigentes ipso facto a Codice Iuris Canonici excerptae* (2. ed., Patavii: Typis Seminarii, 1921), n. 47e (hereafter cited *Censurae vigentes*).

[68] *Commentarium in Codicem Iuris Canonici ad usum Scholarum* (8 vols. in 5, Taurinorum Augustae: Marietti, 1920-1930), lib. V, pars III, n. 148 (hereafter cited *Commentarium*).

[69] *AAS* XXXIV (1942), 22; Bouscaren, *The Canon Law Digest, II,* 286.

Education outside the Catholic Church does not necessarily mean only an education in schism or heresy, although some authors insist that it does.[70] There is no such restriction in the canon itself. Hence the penalty is likewise incurred by the Catholic party who enters marriage with the agreement that some or all of the children will be educated without any religion at all or in an anti-religious sect.[71]

Grave fear excuses from this penalty.[72]

3. Baptism by a non-Catholic minister

Catholics who knowingly presume to offer their children to non-Catholic ministers to be baptized incur automatically an excommunication reserved to the ordinary.[73]

Any Catholic who violates this penal law incures the censure. It makes no difference whether the marriage is entirely Catholic or mixed, or whether there is no marriage at all. It matters not whether the children are legitimate or illegitimate.[74] It makes no difference whether the baptism is administered validly or invalidly, solemnly or privately.[75]

To fall under the censure, however, Catholics must offer their *own* children to be baptized by a non-Catholic minister.[76] The words of the canon must be literally fulfilled. Hence a Catholic midwife does not incur the excommunication of this particular canon if she gives the child of her patient to a non-Catholic minister to be baptized.[77] Neither is the penalty incurred by a Catholic parent who offers his or her child for baptism to a non-Catholic who is not a minister.[78] A

70 Cf., e.g., Cocchi, *loc. cit.*

71 Cf. Coronata, *Institutiones,* IV, 326; Sipos, *Enchiridon Iuris Canonici,* p. 553.

72 Cappello, *De Censuris,* n. 371.

73 Canon 2319, § 1, 3°.

74 Cf. Cipollini, *De Censuris,* n. 72; Cappello, *De Censuris,* n. 372.

75 Cappello, *loc. cit.*

76 Cf. Sipos, *Enchiridion Iuris Canonici,* p. 553, nota 14.

77 Cappello, *loc. cit.*

78 Coronata, *Institutiones,* IV, 327.

Catholic parent—and this could happen in the case of a mixed marriage—is not excommunicated if he or she merely allows the child to be offered to a non-Catholic minister for baptism. [79] Finally, this excommunication is not incurred by Catholic parents who offer their children to a non-Catholic minister to be confirmed or to receive communion. [80]

Inasmuch as canon 2319, § 1, 3°, the particular canon under discussion, contains the phrase "who knowingly presume," certain conditions must be verified before the penalty of excommunication can be incurred. The offender must know of the the prohibition, he must know of the specific censure inflicted for its violation, he must know that the person to whom he is offering his child for the administration of baptism is a non-Catholic minister. [81] Any ignorance, less than affected ignorance, of these points, any degree of force or fear, anything at all that diminishes full imputability ever so slightly, excuses the offender from incurring this particular censure. Of course, necessity or danger of death always excuses; in such cases anyone may baptize. [82]

4. Education in a non-Catholic religion

An excommunication, reserved to the ordinary, is automatically incurred by any Catholic parent or parents who knowingly send their children to be educated or instructed in a non-Catholic religion. [83] Not only the Catholic parents, but likewise those who take their place are subject to this censure. [84] The penalty, therefore, can be incurred by those who are legally appointed as gaurdians of the children; by grandparents, immediate members of the family, relatives or others

[79] Cf. Cipollini, *De Censuris*, n. 72.

[80] Cavigioli, *De Censuris latae sententia quae in Codicis Iuris Canonici continentur Commentariolum* (Torino: Libreria Editrice Internazionale, 1918), n. 157 (hereafter cited *De Censuris*).

[81] Cocchi, *Commentarium*, lib. V, pars III, n. 149; Coronata, *Institutiones*, IV, 327.

[82] Cf. Cipollini, *De Censuris*, n. 72.

[83] Canon 2319, § 1, 4°.

[84] Canon 2319, § 1, 4°.

who undertake to care for the children when the parents are unable to do so or are deceased; and by the directors of the schools to whom the children are entrusted.[85]

It is necessary to take note of the fact that the canon forbids under excommunication the *non-Catholic religious education* of the children; the canon itself does not legislate concerning the education given by non-Catholics in other branches of learning.[86] Hence, if the education or instruction is not in a non-Catholic religion, it is not included under this section of the penal canon, no matter by whom it is given.[87]

The canon uses the word "knowingly." As in the precedlng case,[88] so in this instance a full knowledge of the law, of the censure, and of the facts is presupposed before the penalty can be incurred.[89] Ignorance, even crass or supine, force or fear in any degree, any cause that diminishes imputability, is sufficent to excuse a person from incurring the penalty.

5. False relics

An automatic excummunication, reserved to the ordinary, is incurred by a person who makes false relics or who knowingly sells them, distributes them, or exposes them to the public veneration of the faithful.[90]

The canon explicitly mentions four different delicts relative to false relics, each of which is penalized with an excommunication.[91] It will suffice here to take note of two points. First, with reference to the exposition alone, anyone who exposes false relics to the *private*

---

[85] Coronata, *Institutiones*, IV, 327; cf. Cipollini, *De Censuris*, n. 73.

[86] Cf. Cavigioli, *De Censuris*, n. 158; Cheodi, *Ius Poenale*, n. 60 ad 7; Cocchi, *Commentarium*, lib. V, pars III, n. 150.

[87] The sending of children to public schools in the United States is not included under the censure of canon 2319, § 1, 4^{0}; it is, however, prohibited by canon 1374.—Ramstein, *Manual*, p. 709.

[88] Cf. *supra*. p. 94.

[89] Cocchi, *loc. cit.*

[90] Canon 2326.

[91] Coronata, *Institutiones*, IV, 352.

but not *public,* veneration of the faithful, does not incur the penalty.[92] Secondly, with reference to the sale, distribution ,and exposition of the false relics, full knowledge and imputability is necessary in order that the penalty be incurred. Therefore, anything at all that diminishes the imputability likewise excuses the person from incurring the censure.

6. Violation of the privilege of the canon

An excommunication, reserved to the proper ordinary, is incurred automatically by a person who inflicts any real injury on the person of clerics of rank inferior to bishops or on the person of religious of either sex.[93]

The object of the injury can be the body, the liberty, or the dignity of the cleric or religious. The act, however, must of its nature be malicious. Hence, no censure is incurred, if, for example, a cleric is struck in a joking way, or in defence of one's own or another's life, possessions, or virtue, when these are threatened, or if the injury is inflicted in the spirit of chastisement by one in authority.[94]

The excommunication is reserved to the ordinary of the guilty person who inflicts the injury.[95] It is here that a distinction seems necessary in reference to the Regular confessor's power to grant absolution. If the ordinary in a particular case is the local ordinary, the Regular can absolve from the censure; if, however, the ordinary is a major superior in an exempt clerical institute, the Regular has no power to grant absolution from the excommunication in virtue of his prvilege.

---

[92] Coronata, *ibid.*, 351; Cipollini, *De Censuris*, n. 75.

[93] Canon 2343, § 4.

[94] Cf. Chelodi, *Ius Poenale*, n. 75; McGrath, *The Privilege of the Canon*, The Catholic University of America Canon Law Studies, n. 242 (Washington, D.C.: The Catholic University of America Press, 1946), pp. 98-110.

[95] McGrath, *op. cit.*, p. 123.

7. Abortion

Those who procure an effective abortion—and the mother is included among them—incur automatically an excommunication reserved to the ordinary.[96]

In the canonical sense abortion signifies the ejection of an immature or non-viable fetus from the womb of the mother.[97] The fetus is termed immature when it cannot live apart from the mother; and this is the case during the six months' period that follows conception. At the beginning of the seventh month the fetus is considered viable.[98]

The procedure of bringing a viable fetus from the womb of the mother prior to the normal time of birth is known as "acceleration of birth"; this does not constitute the crime of abortion for the reason that it is the ejection of a *mature* fetus.[99] Nor are those guilty of the canonical crime of abortion who eject the seed within a period of twenty-four hours after copulation.[100]

The penal canon speaks of those "who procure abortion." This includes anyone who directly intends the abortion and purposely tries to bring it about by means which are in themselves efficacious.[101] The efficaciousness of the means that are used need not be absolute in order that the censure be incurred. A relative efficaciousness—that, namely, which is effective in a particular case, depending upon the condition and constitution of the woman involved—suffices.[102] It matters not whether the means used be physical or moral, simple or complex; all that is required is that they be efficacious.[103]

---

[96] Canon 2350, § 1.

[97] Cavigioli, *De Censuris*, n. 161; Huser, *The Crime of Abortion in Canon Law*, p. 90.

[98] Cocchi, *Commentarium*, lib. V, pars III, n. 198.

[99] Cf. De Meester, *Juris Canonici et Juris Canonico-civilis Compendium* (nova editio, 3 vols. in 4, Brugis: Desclée, 1921-1928), n. 1853 (hereafter cited *Compendium*); Wernz-Vidal, *Ius Canonicum*, VII, n. 472.

[100] Huser, *op. cit.*, p. 97; Ramstein, *Manual*, p. 715.

[101] Cappello, *De Censuris*, n. 384; De Meester, *Compendium*, n. 1853; Huser, *op. cit.*, p. 81.

[102] Huser, *op. cit.*, p. 85.

[103] Cf. Huser, *loc. cit.*: Cappello *loc. cit.*

In order that the censure for the crime of abortion be incurred, four elements must be present: 1) the abortion must be a serious sin, both subjectively and objectively; 2) the abortion must be directly intended, either as an end in itself or as a means to another end; 3) the abortion must really take place; and 4) the abortion must really result from the means that are used and not from some other cause.[104]

If there is any doubt whether the means employed really brought about the abortion or whether the abortion actually took place, the censure is not incurred.[105] The excommunication is not incurred if the abortion is intended indirectly, even though the cause is sinful and the effect foreseen;[106] such could be the case, for example when a husband in a fit of anger strikes his wife who is pregnant, and an abortion occurs.[107] Finally, a mother who procures an abortion from grave fear noes not incur the penalty, even though she commits sin.[108] Grave fear could likewise excuse others involved in the abortion.[109]

The excommunication is incurred by all those co-operators whose help or counsel was necessary for the commission of the crime. If any of these, including the mother, become really repentant of their action before the abortion takes place, they can be absolved by any confessor because there is as yet no censure.. If, however, the abortion later follows necessarily from their action, the censure should be incurred, according to the penal principles.[110] In such a hypothesis, the delinquent, whether the mother or the co-operator, has not fully retracted. Nevertheless, in practice it is safe to hold that such a person does not

[104] Cf. Huser, *op. cit.*, pp. 86, 116, 119, 120-121.

[105] Cappello, *De Censuris*, n. 384.

[106] Huser, *op. cit.*, p. 84.

[107] Cf. Cappello, *loc. cit.*

[108] Cappello, *De Censuris*, n. 385; De Meester, *Compendium*, n. 1853; Cipollini, *De Censuris*, n. 79; Huser, *The Crime of Abortion in Canon Law*, p. 142.

[109] Huser, *loc. cit.*

[110] Canon 2209, § 5: Qui suum influxum in delictum patrandum opportuna retractatione abduxerit plene, ab omni imputabilitate liberatur, etiamsi executor delictum ob alias causas sibi proprias nihilominus patraverit; si non abduxerit plene, retractatio minuit, sed non aufert culpabilitatem.

incur the excommunication afterwards when the abortion actually takes place, for the simple reason that the contumacy which is required for incurring a censure is no longer present.[111]

In consequence of the ruling contained in canon 985, 4°, all those who procure an effective abortion, and all the co-operators in the crime, are irregular *ex delicto.*

8. Apostate religious

A religious who apostatizes from his or her religious institute incurs automatically an excommunication which is reserved to the major superior (in those cases in which an exempt clerical institute is involved) or to the ordinary of the place in which he or she resides (in those cases in which an exempt lay institute or a non-exempt clerical or lay institute is involved.[112]

An apostate from a religious institute is a religious in perpetual vows, whether solemn or simple, who leaves the religious house unlawfully and with the intention of not returning, or who leaves the house lawfully but does not return, for the reason that he intends to withdraw himself from religious obedience; this intention is presumed if the religious does not return within a month and has not at least notified his superior within that time of his intention to return.[113]

Hence the crime of apostasy can be predicated neither of those religious who belong to communities whose members profess only temporary vows nor of those religious who, though members of an Order, have only temporary vows.[114]

In order that the crime of apostasy be actually committed and the censure enacted in the penal canon be thereby incurred, three things are necessary: 1) the religious must be *perpetually* professed; 2) the religious must leave the house unlawfully, either actually or presump-

---

[111] Cappello, *De Censuris*, n. 386; De Meester, *Compendium*, n. 1853; Cocchi, *Commentarium*, lib. V, pars III, n. 200; Cavigioli, *De Censuris*, n. 133.

[112] Cf. canon 2385.

[113] Canon 644, § § 1 and 2.

[114] Chelodi, *Ius Poenale*, n. 101.

tively; and 3) the religious must have the intention of not returning.[115]

Although the religious resides outside the house unlawfully and has the intention of not returning, the crime of apostasy is not then and there committed. Since the very notion of a delict demands that it be external,[116] this intention must be manifested exteriorly.[117]

Here again a distinction must be borne in mind by the Regular confessor relative to the extent of his power to absolve from this excommunication. The Regular *cannot,* in virtue of his privilege alone, remit the penalty incurred by an apostate religious who belongs to an exempt clerical institute. The censure incurred by such an apostate is reserved to the major superior of the guilty religious; the privilege of Regulars does not extend to such cases. However, the Regular confessor can absolve from the excommunication in the following cases: 1) if the apostate is a member of an exempt lay institute; 2) if the apostate is a member of a non-exempt lay institute; [118] and 3) if the apostate is a member of a non-exempt clerical institute. The Regular confessor enjoys jurisdiction over these three cases in virtue of his privilege for the reason that in such instances the penalty is reserved to the ordinary of the place wherein the apostate happens to be at the time of his confession.[119]

It is to be noted that the penal canon treats specifically merely of apostates. If there is coupled with this a public apostasy from the Catholic faith, or flight with a member of the other sex, or an attempted marriage, the religious is considered automatically dimissed from

---

115 Cf. Cappello, *De Censuris,* n. 390.

116 Canon 2195: Nomine delicti, iure ecclesiastico, intelligitur externa... legis violatio....

117 Cappello, *loc. cit.*

118 Nuns and sisters, as well as brothers, are here included.

119 "*Ordinario loci, in quo commoratur, reservatam*: in quo scilicet extra domum religiosam illegitime manens, actu, vel transeunter tantum, nullumque ideo habens ibidem domicilium vel quasi-domicilium, exsistit. Quocunque igitur ipse pergat, secum trahit censuram Ordinario loci reservatam."—Cipollini, *De Censuris,* n. 82.

his or her institute,[120] and is subject to the other penalties inflicted according to the nature of the delict. The confessor cannot invoke his privilege to absolve the penitent, except in the case of an attempted marriage; and in this latter case the Regular confessor can absolve a penitent religious then only when the latter *is not in sacred orders and does not have a solemn vow.*[121]

9. Attempted marriage

Religious with perpetual simple vows in an Order or a Congregation who presume to contract marriage, as well as those who presume to contract marriage with them, incur an automatic excommunication reserved to the ordinary.[122]

The words of this canon must be noted with care. The privilege enjoyed by Regulars to absolve from this penalty does *not* extend to clerics or to religious in sacred orders; nor does it include regulars or nuns after they have taken a solemn vow of chasity. If any of the foregoing presume to contract marriage, then they, together with their partners in the delict, incur an automatic *excommunication reserved simply to the Holy See.*[123]

The Regular confessor can invoke his privilege for the benefit only of religious, whether male or female, with perpetual *simple* vows and of those who presume to contract marriage with them. The censure is not incurred by a religious in temporary vows, nor by quasi-religious, that is by those who live the common life after the manner of religious but do not take public vows.[124]

Since only those who *presume* to contract marriage are penalized by the canon, anything that diminishes imputability excuses the religious or his or her accomplice from incurring the censure.

---

[120] Canon 646, § 1.

[121] Cf. *infra*, n. 9.

[122] Canon 2388, § 2.

[123] Canon 2388, § 1.

[124] Cappello, *De Censuris*, n. 395.

10 Violation of the privilege of the forum

A suspension *ab officio,*[125] reserved to the ordinary, is automatically incurred by a cleric who, without the permission of the local ordinary, dares to bring before a lay judge certain persons enjoying the privilege of the forum.[126]

In virture of the privelege of the forum clerics are to be tried in all contentious and criminal cases before an ecclesiastical judge, unless ecclesiastical authority has made provisions to the contrary for particular regions.[127]

To cite clerics before a lay judge is strictly forbidden, unless proper permission has been obtained. The permission of the Holy See is required to summon before a civil court cardinals, papal legates, bishops, abbots or prelates *mullius,* the supreme moderators or generals of religious institutes of pontifical approval, or the major officials of the Roman Curia relative to transactions pertaining to their office.[128]

In order to bring before a lay court as defendants clerics of rank inferior to those just mentioned, permission must be had from the ordinary of the place where the case is tried.[129]

The penalty inflicted for the violation of this prohibition varies according to the dignity of the cleric arraigned before the lay tribunal. If anyone, cleric or lay person, dares to bring before a lay judge a cardinal, a papal legate, a major official of the Roman Curia because of some transaction proper to his office, or his own ordinary, he incurs automatically an excommunication reserved in a special manner to the Holy See.[130]

---

125 A suspension *ab officio* forbids all acts of the power of orders and the power of jurisdiction as well as acts of pure administration connected with the office; the only exception to this prohibition concerns those acts that deal with the administration of the goods of one's own benefice. Cf. canon 2279, § 1.

126 Canon 2341.

127 Canon 120, § 1.

128 Canon 120, § 2.

129 Canon 120, § 2.

130 Canon 2341.

If the person thus brought before the court is any other bishop, or an abbot or prelate nullius, or the supreme moderator or general of a religious institute of pontifical approval, the offender automatically contracts an excommunication reserved simply to the Holy See.[131]

Finally, if the defendant is any other person enjoying the privilege of the forum, the plaintiff, if he be a cleric, incurs automatically a suspension reserved to the ordinary.[132]

It is in reference to this last penalty alone that the Regular confessor can exercise his privilege.

A person becomes a cleric through the reception of first tonsure.[133] All those who have received first tonsure enjoy the privilege of the forum, since this is one of the privileges common to clerics. The privilege is likewise enjoyed by religious, even novices, and even though they are not clerics,[134] and by quasi-religious or those who live the common life but have no public vows.[135]

A cleric, then, who cites a religious or quasi-religious of either sex before a lay court likewise incurs this suspension *ab officio.* Of course, full knowledge and deliberation are required before the penalty is contracted, since the canon speaks of those who "dare" to commit the crime. Hence anything that lessens imputability excuses from the censure.

There is a controversy concerning the identity of the ordinary to whom the suspension is reserved. According to Vermeersch-Creusen the penalty is reserved to the proper ordinary of the offender.[136] A

[131] Canon 2341.

[132] Canon 2341.

[133] Cf. canon 108, § 1.

[134] Canon 614: Religiosi, etiam laici ac novitii, fruuntur clericorum privilegiis de quibus in can. 119-123.

[135] Canon 680: Iidem [i.e., sodales qui vivendi rationem religiosorum imitantur... sed tribus consuetis votis publicis non obstringuntur], etiam laici, gaudent clericorum privilegiis, de quibus in can. 119-123....

[136] *Epitome,* III, n. 540 ad 3. Coronata (*Institutiones,* IV, 431) follows this opinion; Cappello (*De Censuris,* n. 536) terms it the more true one; Beste (*Introductio,* p. 950) calls it the most probable.

Regular confessor, in following this view, could not absolve a guilty religious who belongs to an exempt clerical institute, for the reason that the censure would be reserved to the major superior.

Cerato maintains that the suspension is reserved to the ordinary in general, and hence absolution can be granted by any ordinary, whether bishop or vicar general.[137]

The Code itself seems to lend its weight to the possible support of both opinions. Canon 2253, 3°, sets forth the general principle that any ordinary can absolve his subjects from a censure reserved to the bishop or ordinary; this favors the view of Vermeersch-Creusen, since the ordinary for exempt clerical religious is the major superior, while the ordinary for others is the local ordinary. The canon proceeds to state, however, that the local ordinary can absolve not only his subjects, but also strangers; and this favors the opinion of Cerato, since an exempt clerical religious can be considered likewise as a stranger in relation to the local ordinary, and hence can be absolved by him.[138]

There seems intrinsic evidence from the canon itself in support of the view that any ordinary can absolve the offender if he can exercise jurisdiction over him. Such being the case, the Regular confessor can use his privilege to absolve any cleric who has violated the particular penal law enacted in canon 2341, as here under discussion. It is always to be understood, of course, that religious who are not clerics are incapable of incurring this suspension.

11. Fugitive religious in sacred orders

A fugitive religious in sacred orders incurs an automatic suspension reserved to his own major superior.[139] This penalty is contracted

[137] *Censurae vigentes*, n. 119e; Cappello (*loc. cit.*) calls this a probable opinion.

[138] Canon 2253, 3°: A censura a *iure reservata*, possunt absolvere ille qui censuram constituit vel cui reservata est, eorumque successores aut competentes superiores aut delegati. Quare a censura reservata *Episcopo* vel *Ordinario*, quilibet Ordinarius absolvere potest suos subitos, loci vero Ordinarius etiam peregrinos....

[139] Canon 2386.

by any fugitive religious in major orders who is a professed member of his institute; it matters not whether the profession is solemn or simple, temporary or perpetual.[140]

A fugitive, according to canon 644, 3°, is one who has left the religious house without the permission of the superior, but has at the same time retained the intention of returning to the religious institute. A fugitive likewise is he who has left the house with permission, but has remained away unlawfully beyond the time extended by the permission. In both cases there must be a notable period of absence without a legitimate permission.

Inasmuch as the Code itself states nothing about the length of time presupposed, recourse must be had to the commentators to determine just how long a religious must be absent unlawfully before he is branded as a fugitive. The authors claim that this length of time must be at least two or three days.[141] Since the more favorable opinion is to be applied in the matter of penalties,[142] it is reasonable to hold that an illegitimate absence of three days is required before the religious is termed a fugitive.[143] Of course, if the constitutions of a religious institute specify a definite time-limit in defining the act by which a member becomes a fugitive, then such constitutions must be followed.[144]

To incur the suspension of canon 2386 it is necessary that the reli-

---

[140] Cappello, *De Censuris*, n. 538; cf. Cocchi, *Commentarium*, lib. V, pars III, n. 262.

[141] Beste, *Introductio*, pp. 437 and 968; De Meester, *Compendium*, n. 1889; Vermeersch-Creusen, *Epitome*, III, n. 590; Creusen, *Religious Men and Women in the Code*, n. 341.

[142] Canon 2219, § 1: In poenis benignior est interpretatio facienda.

[143] Cf. Ramstein, *Manual*, p. 382.

[144] Cf. Ramstein, *loc. cit.* The Constitutions of the Friars Minor, for example, define a fugitive, in relation to the penalties enacted in canon 2386, as one who leaves the house illegitimately and remains outside of obedience under any pretext for more than a natural day, or who has, through his own fault, postponed his return for a natural day after the time for his permission has expired. Cf. *Regula et Constitutiones Generales Fratrum Minorum*, n. 126.

gious be professed and in sacred orders.[145] Hence, if a secular priest or deacon or subdeacon, who was making his novitiate in a religious community for the purpose of becoming a member thereof, should have become a fugitive, he would not incur this penalty, for the simple reason that he is not a professed religious. However, a quasi- religious in sacred orders who is really a member of his community would incur the censure by becoming a fugitive. In a response dated June 2-3, 1918, the Code Commission stated that the penalty of canon 2386 applies to clerical societies without vows in as far as the members live a common life.[146]

Inasmuch as this dissertation advances the proposition that Regulars cannot absolve from any censure reserved to the ordinary if that ordinary is a religious major superior, the inclusion of the penalty of canon 2386 among the censures from which Regulars can absolve in virtue of their privilege may occasion some confusion. The reason for its insertion here is evident, as soon as it is realized that there is a dispute in reference to the major superior to whom the suspension is reserved.

From the viewpoint of the nature of the religious institute, major superiors may be divided into four general classes: 1) the major superior of an exempt clerical institute; 2) the major superior of a non-exempt clerical institute; 3) the major superior of an exempt lay institute; and 4) the major superior of a non-exempt lay institute.

With reference to clerical institutes, the major superior of an exempt institute enjoys jurisdiction over his subjects, while the major superior of a non-exempt institute does not.[147] With reference to any lay institute, the major superior cannot posess jurisdiction, because this is restricted to clerics alone.[148] The act of absolving from a censure

---

[145] Cf. Cappello, *De Censuris*, n. 539.

[146] Cf. *AAS*. X (1918), 347; Bouscaren, *The Canon Law Digest*, I, 860.

[147] Canon 501, § 1: Superiores et Capitula, ad normam constitutionum et iuris communis, potestatem habent dominativam in subditos; in religione autem clericali exempta, habent iurisdictionem ecclesiasticam tam pro foro interno, quam pro externo.

[148] Canon 118: Soli clerici possunt potestatem sive ordinis sive iurisdictionis ecclesiasticae . . . obtinere.

however, is an act of jurisdiction and can be exercised only by him who has the power of jurisdiction.

There is no problem in canon 2386 concerning the major superior of an exempt clerical religious institute, since he has jurisdiction in both the internal and the external forum.[149] A fugitive cleric in sacred orders, then, who belongs to such a community cannot in virtue of the papal privilege be absolved by a Regular confessor.

There does, however, exist a difference of opinion in reference to the non-exempt clerical and to the lay institutes. Vermeersch-Creusen claim that the supension enacted in canon 2386 is actually reserved to the superior in the case of non-exempt clerical institutes, but to the local ordinary in the case of lay institues.[150] Both De Meester[151] and Woywod (1880-1941)[152] concur in this opinion. Other authors[153] maintain that in those cases in which the major superior mentioned in canon 2386 is the superior of a non-exempt clerical or of a lay institute, the provision of canon 2385 is to be applied, namely: the suspension of canon 2386 is reserved to the ordinary of the place in which the fugitive resides.

Both of these opinions are probable,[154] and the absolution will be valid in virtue of canon 209, if it is granted by the proper major superior in the case of a fugitive religious in sacred orders who is a member of a non-exempt clerical religious institute, or by the local ordinary in the case of a fugitive religious in sacred orders who belongs either to a non-exempt clerical institute or to a lay institute.[155]

---

149 Canon 501, § 1.

150 *Epitome,* III, n. 590. This is apparently the opinion of Creusen. Vermeersch seems to have held that in non-exempt clerical institutes and in lay institutes the suspension is reserved to the ordinary of the place where the offender resides.—Cf. *Epitome,* I, n. 825.

151 *Compendium,* n. 1889.

152 *A Practical Commentary on the Code of Canon Law* (revised ed., 2 vols., New York: Wagner, 1944), n. 2242 (hereafter cited *Commentary*).

153 E. g., Chelodi, *Ius Poenale,* n. 101, p. 141, nota 2; Sipos, *Enchiridion Iuris Canonici* p. 408.

154 Beste, *Introductio,* p. 969.

155 Cf. Ramstein, *Manual,* p. 714.

The practical conclusion to be drawn by Regulars relative to the use of their privilege to absolve from the penalty enacted in canon 2386 is as follows: if the fugitive religious in sacred orders belongs to an exempt clerical institute, Regulars cannot absolve him in virtue of their privilege, for the reason that the suspension is reserved to a major superior, who, in this instance, is a religious ordinary; if the fugitive is a member of a non-exempt clerical institute, Regulars can absolve him in virtue of their privilege, for the reason that the suspension is reserved to a major superior, who, in this case—according to a probable opinion—is the ordinary of the place where the fugitive resides; finally, if the fugitive religious in sacred orders is a member of a lay institute, Regulars can absolve him in virtue of their privilege for the reason that the suspenson is reserved to a major superior, who, in this case, is likewise the ordinary of the place where the fugitive resides.

12. Violation of the prohibition concerning ecclesiastical burial

Those who, in violation of canon 1240, § 1, freely give ecclesiastical burial to infidels, to apostates from the faith, to heretics, to schismatics, or to others who are under excommunication or interdict, automatically incur an interdict *ab ingressu ecclesiae,* which is reserved to the ordinary.[156]

According to canon 1240, § 1, the following are to be deprived of ecclesiastical burial unless they have given some signs of repentance before death: 1°. notorius apostates from the Christian faith or notorius members of a heretical or schismatic or masonic sect or of other societies of the same nature; 2°. those who have been excommunicated or interdicted when a condemnatory or a declaratory sentence has intervened; 3°. those who have deliberately committed suicide; 4°. those who have died in a duel or as the result of a wound received therefrom; 5°. those who have ordered that their bodies be given to cremation; 6°. other public and manifest sinners.

It is evident that not all those who are mentioned in canon 1240,

[156] Canon 2339.

§ 1, receive mention likewise in canon 2339. Therefore, although it is a serious sin to give ecclesiastical burial to notorius members of the masonic sect or of other sects of the same nature, to those who have deliberately committed suicide, to those who have died in a duel or from a wound received in a duel, to those who have ordered their bodies to be given to cremation, and to other public and manifest sinners — unless these have given some sign of repentance before death — one who does so does not incur the interdict unless the foregoing have also become excommunicated or interdicted through a condemnatory sentence, or unless the fact of their excommunication or interdict has been established by means of a declaratory sentence.[157]

Furthermore, the individuals to whom ecclesiastical burial is prohibited by the penal law of canon 2339 and the general prohibition of canon 1240, § 1, must be in the same category. In other words, the penal canon includes only infidels, *notorious* apostates from the entire Christian faith, *notorious* heretics or schismatics, and persons under excommunication or interdict *when a condemnatory or a declaratory sentence has intervened.*[158]

The Code itself has determined what is meant by an ecclesiastical burial; it consists in three things, namely, in bringing the body to the church, in performing the rites for the dead over the body in the church, and in burying the body in a place lawfully designated for the deceased faithful.[159] This is the canonical definition of "ecclesiastical burial."

There is a dispute among the authors, however, as to just what this term signifies in canon 2339. Some maintain that the term "ecclesiastical burial" as used in the penal canon is verified merely by the fact that the body is interred in a place lawfully designated for

---

[157] Liuzzi, *De delictis contra auctoritates ecclesiasticas* (Romae: Officium Libri Catholici, 1942), pp. 150-151 (hereafter cited *De delictis*).

[158] Cf. Liuzzi, *op. cit.*, p. 150; Chelodi, *Ius Poenale*, n. 73 ad 6; Coronata, *Institutiones*, IV, 418.

[159] Canon 1204: Sepultura ecclesiastica consistit in cadaveris translatione ad ecclesiam, exsequiis super illud in eadem celebratis, illius depositione in loco legitime deputato fidelibus defunctis condendis.

the burial of the faithful.[160] Others hold, on the contrary, that the three elements mentioned in the definition contained in canon 1204[161] must be verified *simultaneously* with reference to the ecclesiastical burial mentioned in canon 2339, unless due to some extrinsic cause, the transfer of the body or the burial in the designated place is rendered impossible.[162]

The second opinion seems the better one in view of the fact that the canonical definition of ecclesiastical burial calls for the presence of the three elements,[163] and of the principle that in reference to penalties the milder interpretation is to be favored.[164]

From the view point of this second opinion the only persons subject to the penalty of canon 2339 in reference to the automatic interdict are the clerics whose duty it is to perform the ecclesiastical burial in the technical sense.[165] Moreover, only such clerics who violate the prohibition "freely" incur the penalty. A presumptuous character is postulated for the delictual act, and hence any cause that lessens imputability excuses the clerics from contracting the censure.[166]

---

[160] Liuzzi, *De delictis,* pp. 147-149; Vermeersch-Creusen, *Eptome,* III, n. 538; De Meester, *Compendium,* n. 1842; Blat, *Commentarium Textus Codicis Iuris Canonici* (5 vols. in 6, Romae: Collegio "Angelico", 1919-1927), V, n. 180 (hereafter cited *Commentarium*); Beste, *Introductio,* p. 949; Sipos, *Enchiridion Iuris Canonici,* n. 151 ad 4.

[161] I. e., *translatio, exsequiae, depositio.*

[162] Chelodi, *Ius Poenale,* n. 73 ad 6; Cavigioli, *De Censuris,* n. 170; Cerato, *Censurae vigentes,* n. 42; Cappello, *De Censuris,* nn. 401 ad 3 et 485; Woywod, *Commentary,* n. 2194.

[163] Cf. canon 1204.

[164] Cf. canon 2219, § 1.

[165] Cappello, *De Censuris,* n. 485; cf. Coronata, *Institutiones,* IV, 420-421.

[166] Cerato, *Censurae vigentes,* n. 99; Cappello, *loc. cit.;* Coronata, *ibid.,* 420; Cipollini, *De Censuris,* n. 94; the contrary view is held by Liuzzi, *De delictis,* p. 154.

Article 4. Marriage before a non-Catholic minister

According to canon 2319, § 1, 1°, an excommunication, reserved to the ordinary, is automatically incurred by those Catholics who contract marriage before a non-Catholic minister contrary to the prescription of canon 1063, § 1.

The latter canon, 1063, § 1, forbids a couple who are intent upon entering a mixed marriage to approach, whether personally or by proxy, whether before or after the Catholic ceremony, a non-Catholic minister acting as such, for the purpose of giving or renewing matrimonial consent.

There must be some sort of religious ceremony coupled with the action of the minister before the prohibition contained in canon 1063, § 1, is violated. Such a violation seems to be present whenever the minister receives and addresses the couple in a church, or, for that matter, even when he acts thus in a private home and is at the same time garbed in some sort of distinctive religious vestments.[167] If the minister acts merely in the capacity of a civil official, no excommunication is incurred by the Catholic party; if, however, the minister acts simultaneously as both a civil and a religious official, the penalty is incurred.[168]

The meaning of canon 2319, § 1, 1°, is much disputed. Just who are the passive subjects of the censure contained in this penal canon? Is the penalty incurred by two Catholics who attempt marriage before a non-Catholic minister acting as such, or is the penalty restricted to the case of a mixed marriage? Some authors maintain that the censure is restricted only to the marriage of a Catholic and a non-Catholic contracted before a minister. Such is the opinion of Chelodi,[169]

[167] Cappello, *De Sacramentis*, III, Pars I, *De Matrimonio*, n. 317; Wernz-Vidal, *Ius Canonicum*, V, n. 182; Schenk, *The Matrimonial Impediments of Mixed Religion and Disparity of Cult*, The Catholic University of America Canon Law Studies, n. 51 (Washington, D.C.: The Catholic University of America, 1929), p. 259, note 8 (hereafter cited *Mixed Religion*).

[168] Coronata, *Institutiones*, IV, n. 1877.

[169] *Ius Poenale*, n. 60 ad 4, nota 2.

Coronata,[170] Cappello,[171] Woywod,[172] Bouscaren - Ellis,[173] and Leech.[174] Other authors claim the contrary, namely, that the censure is likewise incurred if the parties are both Catholics. Such is the view of Wernz - Vidal,[175] Cipollini,[176] Blat,[177] Cocchi,[178] Augustine,[179] Petrovits,[180] Neuberger,[181] Schenk,[182] and Barrett.[183]

A further question has been raised relative to the marriage of a Catholic with a non-Catholic. Is the penalty restricted to a mixed marriage, that is, to the marriage of a Catholic with a *baptized* non-Catholic, or does it embrace likewise the marriage of a Catholic with an *unbaptized* person? Cerato seems to be the only author who holds that the censure is definitely restricted to a mixed marriage.[184] Cappello, while not accepting this view, admits its probability.[185]

---

170 *Institutiones.* IV, 325.

171 *De Censuris.* n. 369.

172 *Commentary.* n. 2167.

173 *Canon Law, A Text and Commentary* (Milwaukee: Bruce, 1946), pp. 880 and 889.

174 *A Comparative Study of the Constitution* "Apostolicae Sedis" *and the* "Codex Iuris Canonici," The Catholic University of America Canon Law Studies, n. 15 (Washington, D.C.: The Catholic University of America, 1922), p. 93.

175 *Ius Canonicum.* VII, n. 410, nota 7.

176 *De Censuris,* n. 70.

177 *Commentarium,* V, n. 157.

178 *Commentarium.* lib. V, pars III, n. 147.

179 *A Commentary on the New Code of Canon Law,* VIII, 297.

180 *The New Church Law on Matrimony* (2 ed., Philadelphia: McVey, 1926), n. 270.

181 *Canon 6 or the Relation of the Codex Iuris Canonici to Preceding Legislation.* The Catholic University of America Canon Law Studies, n. 44 (Washington, D.C.: The Catholic University of America, 1927), pp. 52-53.

182 *Mixed Religion,* nn. 376-377.

183 *A Comparative Study of the Councils of Baltimore and the Code of Canon Law,* The Catholic University of America Canon Law Studies, n. 83 (Washington, D.C.: The Catholic University of America, 1932), p. 137 (hereafter cited *Councils of Baltimore*).

184 *Censurae vigentes,* p. 93.

185 *De Censuris.* n. 369 ad 4.

It seems that the penalty of excommunication would not be incurred by two Catholics who violate the prescription of canon 1063, § 1, for the reason that this particular canon has reference to a mixed marriage. It can be affirmed that the sin committed by two Catholics who attempt a religious marriage before a non-Catholic minister contains more malice than that which is connoted through the marriage of a Catholic with a non-Catholic in the same circumstances. Nevertheless, the gravity of the sin is not the sole determinant of the penalty. In order that any censure be incurred, not only must there be a serious sin, external and consummated, but there must likewise be a penal sanction attached to the law that is violated. The Church does not inflict a penalty for every grave sin. It is the mind of the legislator, in imposing penalties, to prevent and to cure abuses. Certainly the grave danger existed, and continues to exist, in view of statistical frequency, of participation in a non-Catholic religion by attempted marriage before a non-Catholic minister in the case of a mixed marriage; but the marriage of two Catholics before a non-Catholic minister would be something comparatively rare. Hence the Church penalizes the former, while she does not inflict a censure on the latter.

Added to this is the fact that the Code itself demands a strict interpretation in the matter of penalties,[186] and sets forth the fundamental principle that a penalty enacted by the law is not incurred unless the committed delict is perfectly included within the meaning of the words of the law.[187]

Since, therefore, canon 2319, § 1, 1°, explicitly refers only to those who violate canon 1063, § 1, and since the later canon explicitly speaks only of a mixed marriage, it seems that the correct view—a view based on both reason and the principles of law—is that which exempts two Catholics from incurring the penalty of excommunication inflicted for the violation of the penal law contained in canon 2319, § 1, 1°.

---

[186] Canon 19: Leges quae poenam statuunt...strictae subsunt interpretationi.

[187] Canon 2228: Poena lege statuta non incurritur, nisi delictum fuerit in suo genere perfectum secundum proprietatem verborum legis.

The application of the penal principles of the Code seems likewise to exclude any Catholic who marries an *unbaptized* non-Catholic before a non-Catholic minister.[188] It is true that canon 1071 legislates to the effect that whatever is stated in canons 1060-1064 relative to mixed marriages must also be applied to disparate marriages. However, no mention of any censure is made in canons 1060-1064. The penalty is contained in canon 2319, § 1, 1°, and is *explicitly* referred to canon 1063, § 1. To extend this penalty in such wise that it includes not only mixed, but likewise disparate, marriages, seems a violation of the principle contained in canon 2219, § 3.[189] Canon 2319, § 1, 1° refers only to Catholics who give or renew their matrimonial consent with a *baptized* non-Catholic before a non-Catholic minister acting in a religious capacity.

This conclusion, of course, means only that the general law of the Church does not include in its censure the marriage of two Catholics or of a Catholic and an unbaptized person before a non-Catholic minister acting as such. It is still possible for those who are guilty of such a sin to be penalized by particular law. And such a law has been enacted for the Catholics of the United States. The III Plenary Council of Baltimore (1884) decreed an excommunication, reserved to the ordinary, against all Catholics of the United States who contracted or attempted marriage before a non-Catholic minister.[190]

It is true that in virtue of canon 6, 5°, any penalty that is not mentioned in the Code, even though it had been contained in the earlier

[188] Cf. Cerato, *Censurae vigentes,* p. 93.

[189] Cf. *supra,* p. 89.

[190] N. 127: Item decernimus Catholicos, qui coram ministro cuiuscumque sectae acatholicae matrimonium contraxerint vel attentaverint, extra propriam dioecesim, in quolibet statu vel territorio sub ditione praesulum qui huic concilio adsunt vel adesse debent, excommunicationem incurrere episcopo reservatam, a qua tamen quilibet dictorum ordinariorum sive per se, sive per sacerdotem ad hoc delegatum absolvere poterit. Quod si in propria dioecesi ita deliquerint, statuimus eos ipso facto innodatos esse excommunicatione, quae, nisi absque fraude legis alium episcopum adeant, eorum ordinario reservatur.—*Acta et Decreta Concilii Plenarii Baltimorensis Tertii, A. D. MDCCCLXXXIV* (Baltimorae: Typis Ioannis Murphy et Sociorum, 1886).

law, is abrogated.[191] This legislation, however, refers to penalties contained in the general law. It does not in any way abrogate the punishments enacted by particular law unless they are contrary to the Code. The excommunication inflicted by the III Plenary Council of Baltimore against Catholics who attempt marriage before a non-Catholic minister is particular legislation and is not contrary to the Code;[192] it goes beyond the Code, and hence continues to exist.[193]

In virtue of his apostolic privilege a Regular confessor has no jurisdiction to absolve from particular penalties that are reserved by particular law. Nevertheless, it should be noted that there is sufficient extrinsic authority to warrant the view that the marriages of two Catholics and of a Catholic and an unbaptized person are likewise envisioned by canon 2319, § 1, 1⁰.[194] Such an opinion is at least solidly probable.

If this opinion is accepted—and it can be used—it follows that the same delict is punished with the same penalty by both particular and general law. But, according to the present penal law, if different superiors punish the same delict with *different censures* that are automatically incurred, then indeed the automatic censure is multiplied if the delict is committed once or several times.[195] From this canon

---

[191] Canon 6, 5⁰: Quod ad poenas attinet, quarum in Codice nulla fit mentio, spirituales sint vel temporales, medicinales vel, ut vocant, vindicativae, latae vel ferendae sententiae, eae tanquam abrogatae habeantur.

[192] Since, however, the reservation of a censure in a particular territory has no force, according to canon 2247, § 2, outside the limits of that territory, that section of the Baltimore decree which reserves the excommunication as a rule to their own ordinary if the Catholics contract or attempt marriage before a non-Catholic minister *in their own diocese* is contrary to the Code, and hence is abrogated. Cf. canon 6, 1⁰. Any ordinary, therefore, can absolve his subjects from the censure, and a local ordinary can do the same for strangers in the diocese. Cf. Bouscaren-Ellis, *Canon Law, A Text and Commentary*, p. 887.

[193] Cf. Vermeersch-Creusen, *Epitome*, I, n. 78; Beste, *Introductio*, pp. 58 and 939; Bouscaren-Ellis, *op. cit.*, pp. 880 and 889; Barrett, *Councils of Baltimore*, pp. 137-138; Ramstein, *Manual*, pp. 708-709; Mahoney, *The Sacraments*, q. 342, p. 382.

[194] Cf. *supra*, p. 112.

[195] Canon 2244, § 2, 3⁰: Censura latae sententiae multiplicatur: Si delictum, diversis censuris a distinctis Superioribus punitum, semel aut pluries committatur.

some authors have concluded that if the same delict is punished *with the same censure* by both particular and general law, the offender is punished *only* in consequence of the sanction contained in the general law.[196] The general law supplants the particular, and the latter loses its binding force.

From this viewpoint, then, there is no need of the penalty inflicted by the III Plenary Council upon Catholics who contract marriage before a non-Catholic minister, because, under the given hypothesis, the Code has already legislated for that offense.

Hence a Regular confessor can use his privilege to absolve from the excommunication inflicted by canon 2319, § 1, 1°, regardless of whether the offenders are two Catholics, or whether the one is a Catholic and the other is a baptized non-Catholic, so that the case is that of a mixed marriage, or whether the one is a Catholic and the other is a non-baptized non-Catholic, so that the case is that of a disparate marriage.

The Regular confessor, however, cannot in virture of this privilege grant absolution from the automatic excommunication inflicted by the III Plenary Council of Baltimore (1884) upon Catholics who dare to attempt marriage after having obtained a civil divorce.[197] The absolution from this censure is reserved to the ordinary, and the Regular confessor can absolve from it only in urgent cases by the use of canon 2254. It should be noted that the penal law enacted by the Council contains the words "*ausi fuerint.*" Hence any diminution of imputability excuses the offender from contracting the censure.[198]

---

[196] Chelodi, *Ius Poenale*, n. 32, p. 40, nota 1; De Meester, *Compendium*, n. 1734.

[197] *Acta et Decreta Concilii Plenarii Baltimorensis Tertii A. D. MDCCCLXXXIV*, n. 124.

[198] Bouscaren-Ellis, *Canon Law, A Text and Commentary*, p. 906.

CHAPTER V

THE REGULAR CONFESSOR AND THE RESERVATION OF SINS

Priests Regular, once they have been properly presented to the local ordinary by their proper superiors, should not be denied jurisdiction, unless a grave reason justifies such action.[1] The local ordinary may, however, place restrictions upon the jurisdiction which he delegates; but even here he is urged not to restrict the jurisdiction unduly without a reasonable cause.[2] One such type of limitation imposed by the local ordinary is known as the reservation of sins.

By the reservation of cases is meant the withdrawal of a sin or a censure to the judgment of the one making the reservation, so that no one can validly grant absolution except the one who makes the reservation, his successor in office, his superior, or his delegate.[3] The reservation immediately and primarily affects the confessor, for the reason that it limits his power, only mediately and indirectly does it affect the penitent, in so far as the latter must go to the superior for absolution.[4]

---

1 Cf. canons 874, § 2, and 877.

2 Canon 878, § § 1 and 2. In virtue of this canon the religious superior may restrict the *permission* which he grants to his subjects for the act of exercising confessional jurisdiction. The present chapter is concerned only with the limitations placed on the faculties of the confessor by the local ordinary.

3 "Reservatio casum est avocatio alicuius casus (peccati vel censurae) and proprium tribunal reservantis, ita ut nemo absolutionem impertire valeat nisi ipse reservans, eius successor aut superior in officio vel eius delegatus."—Pruemmer, *Manuale Theologiae Moralis* (4 et 5. ed., 3 vols., Friburgi Brisgoviae: Herder, 1928), III, n. 418. Cf. canon 893, § § 1-3.

4 Pruemmer, *loc. cit.*

A case reserved *ratione censurae* is called a reserved censure; a case reserved *ratione peccati* is called a reserved sin.[5] In either case, whether the sin or the censure is reserved, the purpose of withdrawing the power to grant absolution and of reserving that right and power to a higher superior seems to be the same, namely to deter the faithful from committing the more heinous sins, and thus to root up the practice whereby the commission of such sins had become entrenched or even deep-rooted among the faithful.

Local ordinaries, with the exception of the vicar general unless he have a special mandate, certainly have the power to reserve sins.[6] They are, however, forbidden to do so unless the reservation is really necessary or useful.[7] The Code admonishes them to limit the number of reserved sins to three or four of the more grave and atrocious crimes, and to allow even these reservations to remain in force only so long as such action is necessary to root out some deep-rooted vice or to restore Christian discipline when perhaps it had broken down.[8]

If the local ordinary has reserved a sin, the Regular confessor cannot, in virtue of the general faculties received from that ordinary, absolve from the sin. He may do so if the ordinary has likewise granted him the facutly to absolve from the reserved sin; otherwise he must apply to the competent authority for the faculty to impart absolution.

The Code itself has made certain concessions in this matter. Pastors, and those in law equivalent to pastors, can, during the time established for the fulfillment of the paschal Communion, absolve from any sin reserved by the ordinary.[9] If the time for the fulfillment of this precept has been extended by the local ordinary in virtue of the power given to him by the general law[10] or by indult,[11] the faculty

[5] Pruemmer, *op. cit.*, III, n. 419.

[6] Cf. canon 893, § 1.

[7] Canon 895.

[8] Canon 897.

[9] Canon 899, § 3.

[10] The Code, while it defines the period for the fulfillment of the paschal precept as extending from Palm Sunday to Low Sunday nevertheless gives to the local ordinary the right to extend it from the fourth Sunday of Lent to Trinity

whereby the pastor is empowered to absolve, during the period defined for the reception of the paschal communion, from sins reserved by the ordinary is likewise extended to coincide with the time established by the latter.[12]

All missionaries possess the faculty by law to absolve from any sin reserved by the ordinary, that is, during the time in which they are giving a mission to the faithful.[13] Retreat masters are considered the equivalent of missionaries in the use of this faculty.[14]

The Code, besides the concessions it has made in the matter of granting absolution from reserved sins, has likewise established definite occasions on which the reservation ceases, so that absolution can be imparted by any confessor with diocesan faculties. Thus, the reservation ceases in the case of sick people who cannot leave the house for the purpose of confessing their sins, and of those about to be married, when they make their confession in preparation for marriage. This is likewise the case whenever the competent superior has been asked for the faculty to absolve from the reserved sin in some particular case and has refused to grant it, or whenever the confessor prudently judges that he cannot ask the superior for the faculty, for the reason that the penitent will suffer a grave inconvenience or that the sacramental seal will be endangered.[15]

The judgement regarding the grave inconvenience suffered by the penitent devolves entirely upon the confessor. Instances of such difficulties can be multiplied. Grave inconvenience is verified, for ex-

---

Sunday, if circumstances warrant such an extension.—Cf. canon 859, § 2.

[11] Such an indult is in effect in the United States. "In virtue of an indult granted by the Holy See to the United States and promulgated in the II Plen. Council of Baltimore, n. 257, our Easter season extends from the *first Sunday* of Lent to Trinity Sunday unless the local ordinary for good reason deems it expedient to restrict the indult. In virtue of c. 4 of the Code this privilege remains even today."—Ramstein, *Manual*, p. 421.

[12] Cf. Coronata, *De Sacramentis*, I, 427.

[13] Canon 899, § 3.

[14] Cf. Coronata, *loc. cit.*

[15] Canon 900, 1° and 2°.

ample, if the penitent has journeyed a great distance to make this confession; if the penitent finds it very difficult, for any reason, to return to the confessor; if the confessor has reason to fear that the penitent will not return and will thus omit his or her Easter duty; if the penitent will—or it is even feared that he will—suffer the loss of reputation, because of the necessity for having recourse for the faculty; if scandal is feared; if it is very difficult for the penitent to remain in sin during the period of time required to ask for and obtain the faculty to absolve.[16] In these and similar instances, the penitent will suffer grave inconvenience. The reservation, therefore, ceases by law and the confessor can grant absolution.

Finally, the reservation exercises no force outside the territory of the one who makes it, even if the penitent deliberately leaves that territory for the sole purpose of obtaining absolution elsewhere.[17]

The foregoing remarks have dealt with the power of the local ordinary to restrict the jurisdiction of the confessor by reserving sins to his own tribunal. There remains for consideration the problem whether any restrictions are placed on this *episcopal power itself*. In particular, there has arisen the question whether the local ordinary can validly reserve to himself *ratione peccati* a sin which is already reserved to him *ratione censurae* by the general law. The solution of the problem is of importance to the Regular confessor, for it is concerned with the exercise of his privilege to absolve from such censures.[18]

The question has occasioned a rather lengthy controversy.[19] Two

[16] Coronata, *De Sacramentis*, I, 430.

[17] Canon 900, 3°.

[18] These censures have been mentioned and discussed in the preceding chapter.

[19] For an orderly presentation and treatment of the dispute confer the following: "Absolutio a Censuris Papalibus Ordinariis Reservatis"—*The Ecclesiastical Review*, LXVII (1922), 518-522 (hereafter cited *ER*); Vitali, "De Absolutione a Censuris Papalibus Ordinariis Reservatis deque Regularium Privilegio ab iisdem Absolvendi"—*The Homiletic and Pastoral Review*, XXIII (1923), 1284-1285 (hereafter cited *HPR*); idem, "De Mixtis Reservationibus"—*ER*, LXXI (1924), 517-520; "Cases Reserved by Code and by Ordinary"—*ER*, LXXXIV (1931), 190-192; Woywod, "Reservation by

contrary opinions have been offered as a solution of the question. The one, the negative opinion, maintains that the ordinary can never reserve to himself under any aspect, not even *ratione peccati,* the censures reserved to him by the general law. Consequently, Regular confessors can validly and licitly absolve from these particular censures in the sacramental forum, even though the ordinary has reserved them to himself *ratione peccati.* [20] The other, the affirmative opinion, claims that the local ordinary can validly—though not always licitly—reserve to himself *ratione peccati* any of the censures reserved to him by the general law. Consequently, Regulars cannot use their privilege to absolve from such a censure when the ordinary has reserved it to himself *ratione peccati.* [21]

It seems that a solution to this question is to be obtained, not by means of an appeal to the authors, but only through a correct interpretation of canon 898 together with the application of canonical principles. The answer to the problem hinges on the interpretation of canon 898.

Canon 898 may be translated to read as follows:

"All those [i.e., who have the power to reserve sins] shall absolutlely abstain from reserving to themselves those sins which

---

Local Ordinaries of Sins Punished with a Censure in the Common Law"—*HPR,* XXXI (1931), 869-870; Vitali, "Adhuc de Mixtis Reservationibus"—*ER,* LXXXV (1931), 73-75; "Reply to Father Vitali's Objections"— *ibid.,* 75-82; Vitali, "Utrum Locorum Ordinarii Valeant Suspendere Privilegium Regularium 'Absolvendi a Casibus Papalibus Ordinariis Reservatis' per accidens et via exceptionis"—ER, LXXXVI (1932), 292-296; "Reply to Fr. Vitali's Renewed Objections"—*ibid.,* 297-305. Vitali again presented and discussed the matter in an article entitled "De reservationibus pontificiis a iure reservatis ordinario deque Regularium privilegio ab iisdem absolvedi"—*CpR,* XIV (1933), 287-294, 363-375, 436-447; *CpRM,* XVI (1935), 164-175. A solution is likewise attempted by Shuhler, *Privileges of Regulars,* pp. 100-108.

20 Cf. Vitali, "art. cit."—*CpR,* XIV (1933), 288.

21 "Reply to Father Vitali's Objections"—*ER,* LXXXV (1931), 82. In *ER* the controversy was carried on between Vitali and an anonymous writer. Vitali himself indicates that the anonymous writer was Doctor Schaaf. Cf. Vitali, "art. cit."—*CpRM,* XVI (1935), 164.

have already been reserved to the Apostolic See even by reason of a censure, and they shall as a rule abstain from reserving to themselves those sins also to which a censure, though not reserved to anyone, is attached by law." [22]

While this canon is not physically divided into sections or numbers, it can be seen at a glance that it consists logically of two thoughts or ideas. First of all, those inferior to the Holy See are to abstain *absolutely* from reserving to themselves any sin already reserved in any way to the Holy See. It is sufficient to note here that the more common opinion maintains that a violation of this prohibition imports not only an illict, but likewise an invalid act. [23] The basis for this statement is particularly the fact that the word which is used for giving expression to the *absolute prohibition* [24] is considered the equivalent of an invalidating clause. [25]

In its second part, canon 898 commands inferiors to abstain *regularly* from reserving to themselves sins to which the law has annexed a censure, even though the censure is not reserved to anyone. It is this second expressed concept that seems to present the greatest difficulty.

It is an established canonical principle that ecclesiastical laws are to be interpreted according to the proper signification of the words as considered in their text and context. [26] In view of this principle it is evident that the first clause of canon 898 has reference to cases reserved *to* the Apostolic See. It is likewise evident that the second clause of the canon includes at least the non-reserved censures.[27]

---

[22] Canon 898: Prorsus ab iis peccatis sibi reservandis omnes abstineant quae iam sint Sedi Apostolicae etiam ratione censurae reservata, et regulariter ab iis quoque quibus censura, etsi nemini reservata, a iure imposita sit.

[23] "Reply to Father Vitali's Objections"—ER, LXXXV (1931), 77; Shuhler, *Privileges of Regulars,* p. 102.

[24] The Latin term is "*prorsus.*"

[25] Canon 11: Irritantes aut inhabilitantes eae tantum leges habendae sunt, quibus aut actum esse nullum aut inhabilem esse personam expresse vel aequivalenter statuitur. Cf. *ER, loc. cit.*

[26] Canon 18.

[27] *Censurae nemini reservatae.*

But what about the censures that are reserved to the ordinary by the general law? These seem to be definitely excluded from consideration in the first clause of canon 898 in view of the fact that in this clause mention is specifically and explicitly made only of cases reserved *to,* not *by*, the Holy See. Are they to be considered as mentioned by the legislator in the second clause of the canon? The historical antecedents and the textual construction of this second clause can lead to only one conclusion, namely, that the second part of canon 898 *cannot* be interpreted in such a way as to connote also an implicit mention of censures reserved by law to any authority intermediate to the Holy See.

Canon 898 has been taken, practically word for word, from an Instruction issued by the Holy Office on July 13, 1916. [28] According to this Instruction, ordinaries were to abstain entirely from reserving to themselves sins which had already been reserved to the Apostolic See, so that laws would not be multiplied without necessity; and these same ordinaries were to abstain regularly from reserving to themselves sins to which a censure, though not reserved to anyone, had been attached by law. [29]

In reference to this latter part of the prohibition, the Holy Office went on to state that an Instruction issued on November 26, 1602, by the Sacred Congregation of Bishops and Regulars had expressly forbidden it. [30] What was it that the Sacred Congregation of Bishops and Regulars had expressly forbidden? That ordinaries should not regularly reserve to themselves cases other than those already reserved by and to the Holy See and of which non-reserved censures were but an example? That ordinaries should not regularly reserve to them-

[28] S. C. S. Off., instr. 13 iul. 1916, n. 4—*Fontes,* n. 1302.

[29] "Prorsus autem ab iis peccatis sibi reservandis Ordinarii abstineant, quae iam sint Sedi Apostolicae reservata, ne scilicet absque necessitate multiplicentur leges; et, regulariter, ab iis quoque quibus censura, etsi nemini reservata, a iure imposita sit..."—S. C. S. Off., instr., *loc. cit.*

[30] "...hoc enim expresse prohibet vetus Instructio S. Congregationis Episcoporum et Regularium diei 26 novembris 1602..."—S. C. S. Off., instr., *loc. cit.*

selves the absolution of sins to which were attached either censures not reserved to anyone or censures reserved to them by the general law? No. The Sacred Congregation of Bishops and Regulars explicitly mentioned *only* the censures that were not reserved to anyone, and these were the censures that ordinaries were forbidden to reserve, as a rule, to themselves.[31]

There can be no doubt that the Sacred Congregation of Bishops and Regulars spoke only of non-reserved censures in the above-mentioned portion of the Instruction issued on November 26, 1602. There can be no doubt that the Supreme Congregation of the Holy Office had in mind only non-reserved censures in the second part of the Instruction issued on July 13, 1916—and this despite the fact that the particle *etsi* was used in place of the pronoun *cuius*—because of the fact that the Holy Office incorporated the very words of the Sacred congregation of Bishops and Regulars to explain the meaning of its prohibition. Finally, there can be no doubt that canon 898, inasmuch as it incorporates the text of the Holy Office, contemplates mention solely of non-reserved censures in its second clause.

Hence it seems altogether logical to conclude that those censures which are reserved to the ordinary by the general law are simply left unmentioned in canon 898. But unless these censures, as well as those that are non-reserved, are given mention in the second part of canon 898, will not one be forced to admit that there is a *lacuna* in the law?[32] Is there anything wrong in such an admission? Let it be supposed that there is a *lacuna* in the law. There is nothing strange about that, inasmuch as the legislator himself has made provisions for just such difficulties. Provisions for *lacunae* in the law are contained in canon 20. This canon states that if there is lacking any express prescription

---

[31] "... hoc enim expresse prohibet vetus Instructio S. Congregationis Episcoporum et Regularium diei 26 novembris 1602, quae ita se habet: 'Praesertim vero haec monenda censet Sacra Congregatio, ut videant ipsi Ordinarii ne illos casus promiscue reservent quibus adnexa est excommunicatio major a iure imposita, cuius absolutio nemini reservata sit, nisi forte propter frequens scandalum aut aliam necessariam causam aliqui huiusmodi casus nominatim reservandi viderentur.' "—S. C. S. Off., *loc. cit.*

[32] Shuhler, *Privileges of Regulars*, p. 103.

of law, the norm is to be taken, except in the application of penalties, from laws that have been enacted in similar cases; from the general principles of law, tempered with canonical equity; from the style and practice of the Roman Curia; from the common and constant opinion of jurists.[33]

In the problem under discussion, there is no question of applying penalties; there are no laws enacted in similar cases; there is no common and constant opinion of canonical jurists. There are, however, general principles of law that should lead one to a practical and correct solution, and the Holy See itself, in the one and only sin which it has reserved to itself, seems to have committed itself to one mode of procedure rather than another.

It is a general principle of ecclesiastical penal law that whenever a censure which impedes the reception of the sacraments, such as an excommunication, is reserved, the sin to which the censure is attached becomes thereby implicitly reserved.[34] It is likewise a general principle of ecclesiastical penal law that, if the offender is excused from incurring the censure or has been absolved from it, the reservation of the sin ceases in its entirety to exist.[35] This, however, is not the case if the ordinary can reserve to himself a sin to which such a reserved censure has been attached. In this hypothesis the offender would indeed escape the penalty inflicted by the general law, but he would not escape the juridical discrimination resulting from the particular legislation. In such a situation the particular law seems to conflict with and to contradict the general law.[36] But it is not right that an inferior should contradict a higher authority. Therefore the ordi-

[33] Canon 20: Si certa de re desit expressum praescriptum legis sive generalis sive particularis, norma sumenda est, nisi agatur de poenis applicandis, a legibus latis in similibus; a generalibus iuris principiis cum aequitate canonica servatis; a stylo et praxi Curiae Romanae; a communi constantique sententia doctorum.

[34] Canon 2246, § 3.

[35] Canon 2246, § 3.

[36] Cf. Woywod, "Reservation by Local Ordinaries of Sins Punished with a Censure in the Common Law"—*HPR*, XXXI (1931), 868-870.

nary cannot reserve to himself a sin which is already reserved to him in view of the censure as attached by the general law.[37]

In view of this application of principles, it may well be asked whether the same sin can be reserved both *ratione sui* and *ratione censurae* at one and the same time. It seems to be the mind of the Church that this cannot be done within the framework of canonical legislation. The practice of the Holy See seems likewise to favor that viewpoint.

Canon 894 contains the one and only sin reserved to the Holy See. Many authors[38] state that this is the same sin to which there is attached a censure reserved in a special manner to the Holy See by canon 2363. But this view does not seem to be correct.

According to canon 894, the one and only sin reserved *ratione sui* to the Holy See is a false accusation whereby an innocent priest is denounced before ecclesiastical judges for the crime of solicitation[39] Canon 2363, on the other hand, inflicts an automatic excommunication, reserved in a special manner to the Holy See, upon anyone who falsely denounces a confessor to his superiors for the crime of solicitation.[40]

[37] The conflict between the particular and the general law does not exist in the case of the non-reserved censures. There is no such contradiction between the particular and the general legislation when the local ordinary reserves to himself *ratione peccati* the sin to which the general law has already attached a censure not reserved to anyone. Cf. Woywod, "art. cit."

[38] E.g., Chelodi, *Ius Poenale,* n. 88; Vermeersch-Creusen, *Eptome,* III, n. 565; Coronata, *Institutiones,* IV, 522 and 526; Claeys Bouuaert-Simenon, *Manuale Iuris Cannonici,* II, n. 142; Aertnys-Damen, *Theologia Moralis,* II nn. 387 and 430; Augustine, *A Commentary on the New Code of Canon Law,* IV, 318.

[39] Canon 894: Unicum peccatum ratione sui reservatum Sanctae Sedi est falsa delatio, qua sacerdos innocens accusatur de crimine sollicitationis apud iudices ecclesiasticos.

[40] Canon 2363: Si quis per seipsum vel per alios confessarium de sollicitationis crimine apud Superiores falso denuntiaverit, ipso facto incurrit in excommunicationem speciali modo Sedi Apostolicae reservatam, a qua nequit ullo in casu absolvi, nisi falsam denuntiationem formaliter retractaverit, et damna, si qua inde secuta sint, pro viribus reparaverit, imposita insuper gravi ac diuturna poenitentia, firmo praescripto can. 894.

The two canons seem to treat of separate matters: the one speaks of a false denunciation in court, [41] the other treats of a false denunciation to superiors. [42] Hence if a person denounces a priest falsely *before ecclesiastical superiors,* he incurs the reserved censure in consequence of the enactment contained in canon 2363, but the sin is not reserved. On the other hand, if someone denounces a priest falsely *before an ecclesiastical court,* the sin is reserved by force of the ruling contained in canon 894, but the censure as enacted in canon 2363 is not incurred. [43]

This seems a logical conclusion in view of the texts of the canons. It seems at least sufficient to establish a *dubium iuris* regarding the fact whether one and the same sin is contemplated in both canons. It likewise supports the argument that the Holy See apparently does not favor the practice of reserving one and the same sin at one and the same time in a twofold manner, that is, both *ratione peccati* and *ratione censurae.* It lends credence to the view that such a practice is opposed to the principles of canon law.

It may be concluded, therefore, that the ordinary cannot reserve to himself a sin to which there is attached a censure reserved to him by the general law. If the ordinary does do so, the reservation seems invalid and the Regular confessor can disregard it.

This conclusion is supported not only by jurisprudence, but likewise by the external argument from authority. This view is maintained by Coronata, [44] Schaefer, [45] Capobianco, [46] Woywod, [47] and Vitali. [48]

---

[41] Canon 894.

[42] Canon 2363.

[43] Cerato, *Censurae vigentes,* p. 172.

[44] *De Sacramentis,* I, 425.

[45] *De Religiosis,* n. 446c.

[46] *Privilegia,* n. 119.

[47] *Commentary,* n. 809. Cf. also *HPR,* XXI (1931), 869-870.

[48] "De reservationibus pontificiis a iure reservatis ordinario deque Regularium privilegio ab iisdem absolvendi"—*CpR,* XIV (1933), 288.

Shuhler upholds the power of the local ordinary to make such reservations, and states in his conclusions that if the ordinary should do so, the Regular confessor may not impart absolution.[49] In the body of his work, however, he admits the probability of the opposite view, and states that canon 209 will supply the necessary jurisdiction for the validity of the absolution granted by the Regular confessor despite the episcopal reservation.[50]

---

[49] *Privileges of Regulars*, p. 169.

[50] *Ibid.*, pp. 107-108.

CONCLUSIONS

As a consequence of arguments presented in this work, the following conclusions seem justified with regard to the jurisdiction of the Regular confessor:

1. In the Code of Canon Law an approved confessor is always a priest invested with confessional jurisdiction.

2. The confessor who absolves an exempt religious in virtue of diocesan faculties alone cannot, unless he has received a special faculty from the local ordinary, or unless the reservation has ceased according to the tenor of canon 900, nn. 1-3, absolve such a penitent from a sin reserved in the diocese, but he can absolve him from a sin reserved in the exempt religious institute.

3. The confessor who has jurisdiction solely from the competent superior of the penitent exempt religious can absolve him from the diocesan reservation, but cannot impart absolution from sins reserved in the exempt religious institute, unless he has received a special faculty from the competent superior, or unless he is one of the confessors mentioned in canon 518, § 1, to whom the religious is bound to confess regularly.

4. The confessor who possesses simultaneously jurisdiction delegated by both the local ordinary and the competent superior of an exempt religious institute can absolve a penitent exempt religious subject from both the diocesan reservation and the sin reserved in the exempt institute, unless the sin in both instances is identical.

5. For the valid and licit use of the faculty granted by canon 523, in virtue of which any woman religious who is gravely ill can confess to a priest with the jurisdiction necessary for the act of hearing the confessions of women, such a confessor need not possess jurisdiction for hearing the confessions of women from the ordinary of the place where the sick religious goes to confession, but simply jurisdiction for hearing the confessions of women from any local ordinary suffices.

6. A Regular confessor who is on a journey can probably hear the confessions of the faithful validly, provided that he possesses jurisdiction delegated by some local ordinary, that he cannot conveniently for the purpose of obtaining faculties present himself to the ordinary of the place through which he is traveling, and that the pastor is not opposed to his act of hearing the confessions.

7. The Regular confessor can absolve from those automatically incurred censures which are reserved by the Code of Canon Law to the ordinary in all those instances in which the ordinary is likewise the local ordinary. When the grant of absolution is restricted to the major superior of an exempt clerical religious institute, the confessor cannot impart absolution in virtue of his papal privilege; in such cases he can rely on canon 2254.

8. Because of a doubt of law, it may safely be held that the automatic excommunication inflicted by the III Plenary Council of Baltimore upon Catholics who attempt to marry each other before a non-Catholic minister has been superseded by the Code of Canon Law. The Regular confessor, therefore, may use his privilege to absolve such Catholics from this excommunication.

9. The Regular confessor cannot, however, invoke this privilege to absolve a penitent from the automatically incurred excommunication inflicted by the III Plenary Council of Baltimore upon Catholics who dare to attempt marriage after having obtained a civil divorce. In this case, absolution can be granted in virtue of canon 2254 if the case is urgent.

10. In order to use the papal privilege of absolving from automatic censures reserved by the Code to the ordinary, the Regular confessor does not have to possess confessional jurisdiction in his Order. What is necessary is that he possess jurisdiction delegated by the local ordinary for the act of hearing the confessions of the faithful, and that he have at least the presumed permission of his competent superior to exercise this jurisdiction.

11. The local ordinary cannot validly reserve to himself any sin to which there is already attached an automatically incurred censure that is reserved to him by the Code. If the local ordinary does make such a reservation, the Regular confessor can safely grant absolution.

BIBLIOGRAPHY

Sources

Acta Apostolicae Sedis, Romae: Typis Polyglottis Vaticanis, 1909—

Acta et Decreta Concilli Plenarii Baltimorensis Tertii, A. D. MDCCCLXXXIV. Baltimorae: Typis Ioannis Murphy et Sociorum, 1886.

Acta Ordinis Fratrum Minorum, Ad Claras Aquas: Ex Typographia Collegii S. Bonaventurae, 1889—

Acta Sanctae Sedis, 41 vols., Romae, 1865-1908.

Augustinus a Virgine Maria, *Privilegia omnium religiosorum Mendicantium et non Mendicantium,* 3. ed., Lugduni, 1664.

Bouscaren, T. Lincoln, *The Canon Law Digest,* 2 vols., Milwaukee: Bruce, 1934-1943.

Bullarium Franciscanum, editum studio et labore Joannis Hyacinthi Sbaraleae, tomi I-IV, Romae, 1759-1768.

Bullarum Diplomatum et Privilegiorum Sanctorum Romanorum Pontificum Taurinensis editio, 25 vols., Augustae Taurinorum, 1857-1872.

Codex Iuris Canonici Pii X Pontificis Maximi iussu digestus Benedicti Papae XV auctoritate promulgatus, Romae: Typis Polyglottis Vaticanis, 1917.

Codicis Iuris Canonici Fontes cura Emi Petri Card. Gasparri editi, 9 vols., Romae (postea Civitate Vaticana): Typis Polyglottis Vaticanis, 1923-1939. Vols VII-IX ed. cura et studio Emi Iustiniani Card. Serédi.

Confettius, J., *Collectio privilegiorum sacrorum Ordinum Fratrum Mendicantium et non Mendicantium,* Florentiae, 1598.

Corpus Iuris Canonici, editio Lipsiensis secunda post A. Richteri curas instruxit A. Friedberg, 2 vols., Lipsiae, 1879-1881.

Corpus Scriptorum Ecclesiasticorum Latinorum, 71 vols., Vindobonae, 1866—

Decretum Gratiani, emendatum et notationibus illustratum una cum glossis, Gregorii XIII Pont. Max. iussu editum, Romae, 1582.

Denzinger, H. - Bannwart, C. - Umberg, J., *Enchiridion Symbolorum, Definitionum et Declarationum de Rebus Fidei et Morum,* 21.-23. ed., Friburgi Briscoviae: Herder, 1937.

Jaffé, P., *Regesta Pontificum Romanorum ab condita Ecclesia ad annum post Christum natum MCXCVIII,* editionem secundam correctam et auctam auspiciis Gulielmi Wattenbach curaverunt S. Loewenfeld, F. Kaltenbrunner, P. Ewald, 2 vols., Lipsiae, 1885-1888.

Mansi J., *Sacrorum Conciliorum Nova et Amplissima Collectio,* 53 vols. in 60, Parisiis, 1901-1927.

Monumenta Germaniae Historica, Legum Sectio III, *Concilia,* Tomus II, Pars II, recensuit Albertus Werminghoff, Hannoverae et Lipsiae, 1908.

Monumenta Germaniae Historica, Scriptorum Rerum Merovingicarum Tomus IV, *Passiones Vitaeque Sanctorum Aevi Merovingici* edidit Bruno Krusch, Hannoverae et Lipsiae, 1902.

Regula et Constitutiones Generales Fratrum Minorum, Quaracchi: Ex Typographia Collegii S. Bonaventurae, 1922.

Schroeder, H., *Canons and Decrees of the Council of Trent,* St. Louis: Herder, 1941.

Thiel, A., *Epistolae Romanorum Pontificum genuinae et quae ad eos scriptae sunt a S. Hilaro* (461-468) *ad S. Hormisdam* (514-523), Brunsbergae, 1868.

Authors

Aertnys, J. - Damen, C., *Theologia Moralis,* 14 ed., 2 vols., Torino: Marietti . 1944.

Alphonsus Liguori, St., *Theologia Moralis,* edito . . . nova . . . collata . . . recognita. . . . illustrata, cura et studio P. Leonardi Gaudé, 4 vols., Romae: Ex Typographia Vaticana, 1905-1912.

Augustine, C., *A Commentary on the New Code of Canon Law,* 8 vols.: Vols. I-II, 6 ed., 1931-1936; Vols. III, V, 5. ed., 1938; Vols. IV, VI-VIII, 3. ed., 1925-1931, St. Louis: Herder.

A Vasto, B., *De Communicatione Privilegiorum praesertim inter Religiones,* Aquilae, 1936.

Bachofen (Charles Augustine), *Compendium Iuris Regularium*, New York: Benziger, 1903.

Barrett, J., *A Comparative Study of the Councils of Baltimore and the Code of Canon Law*, The Catholic University of America Canon Law Studies, n. 83, Washington, D.C.: The Catholic University of America, 1932.

Berutti, C., *Institutiones Iuris Canonici*, 6 vols., Vols. I, III et VI, Taurini-Romae: Marietti, 1936-1938.

Beste, U., *Introductio in Codicem*, 2. ed., Collegeville, Minn.: St. John's Abbey Press, 1944.

Blat, A., *Commentarium Textus Codicis Iuris Canonici*, 5 vols. in 6, Romae: Collegio "Angelico", 1919-1927.

Bonzelet, H., *The Pastoral Companion*, 9. ed., Chicago: Franciscan Herald Press, 1943.

Bouscaren, T. - Ellis, A., *Canon Law, A Text and Commentary*, Milwaukee: Bruce, 1946.

Browne, A., *Handbook of Notes on Theology*, St. Louis: Redemptorist Fathers, 1944.

Capobianco, P., *Privilegia et Facultates Ordinis Fratrum Minorum*, Salerno: ex conventu S. M. Angelorum, 1946.

Cappello, F., *De Censuris*, 2. ed., Taurinorum Augustae: Marietti, 1925.

———*Tractatus Canonico-Moralis de Sacramentis*, 3 vols. in 6, Romae: Marietti, 1935-1945. Vol. III, partes I et II, *De Matrimonio*, 4. ed., 1939; Vol. II, *De Poenitentia*, 4. ed., 1944.

Cavigioli, I., *De Censuris latae sententiae quae in Codicis Iuris Canonici continentur Commentariolum*, Torino: Libreria Editrice Internazionale, 1918.

Cerato, P., *Censurae vigentes ipso facto a Codice Iuris Canonici excerptae*, 2. ed., Patavii: Typis Seminarii, 1921.

Chelodi, I., *Ius Poenale et Ordo Procedendi in iudiciis criminalibus iuxta Codicem Iuris Canonici*, 4 ed., Tridenti: Libreria Moderna Editrice A. Ardesi, 1935.

Cipollini, A., *De Censuris Latae Sententiae iuxta Codicem Iuris Canonici*, Taurini: Marietti, 1925.

Claeys Bouuaert, F. - Simenon, G., *Manuale Iuris Canonici*, 3 vols.: Vol. I, 4. ed., 1934; Vol. II, 2. ed., 1935; Vol. III, 3. ed., 1931, Gandae et Leodii: apud auctores, 1931-1935.

Cocchi, G., *Commentarium in Codicem Iuris Canonici ad usum Scholarum*, 8 vols. in 5, Taurinorum Augustae: Marietti, 1920-1930.

Coronata, a, M., *De Sacramentis Tractatus Canonicus*, 3 vols., Taurini-Romae: Marietti, 1943-1946.

——*Institutiones Iuris Canonici*, 2. ed., 5 vols., Taurini: Marietti, 1939-1947.

Cotinio, A., *Summa Diana*. Venetiis, 1668.

Creusen, J., *Religious Men and Women in the Code*, 4. Eng. ed., revised and edited to conform with the 5. French edition, by Adam C. Ellis; first translation by Edward F. Garesché, Milwaukee: Bruce, 1940.

Dawson, C., *The Making of Europe*, New York: Sheed and Ward, 1945.

De Meester, A., *Juris Canonici et Juris Canonico-civilis Compendium*, nova editio, 3 vols. in 4, Brugis: Desclée, 1921-1928.

Didacus ab Aragonia, *Dilucidatio Privilegiorum Ordinum Regularium, praesertim Mendicantium*, Bononiae, 1753.

Duchesne, L., *Early History of the Christian Church*, translated from the fourth French edition by Claude Jenkins, 3 vols., London: Murray, 1931-1938.

Elbel, B. - Bierbaum, I., *Theologia Moralis*, 3. ed., 3 vols., Paderbonae, 1904-1907.

Fagnanus, P., *Commentaria in Quinque Libros Decretalium*, 5 libri in 3, Venetiis, 1729.

Fanfani, L., *De Iure Religiosorum*, 2. ed., Taurini-Romae: Maretti, 1925.

Ferraris, L., *Prompta Bibliotheca Canonica, Iuridica, Moralis, Theologica, necnon Ascetica, Polemica, Rubricistica, Historica*, 8 vols., Romae, 1781-1784.

Genicot, E. - Salsmans, J., *Institutiones Theologiae Moralis*, 11. ed., 2 vols., Bruxellis: Dewit, 1927.

Gerster a Zeil, T., *Ius Religiosorum in compendium redactum*. Taurini: Marietti, 1935.

Goyeneche, S., *Iuris Canonici Summa Principia*, Pars II, *De Religiosis*. Romae. Tip. Pol. "Cuore di Maria," 1938.

Guggenberger, A., *A General History of the Christian Era*. 3 vols.: Vol. I, 18. ed., 1931; Vol. II, 16. ed., 1931; Vol. III, 13 ed., 1928, St. Louis: Herder, 1928-1931.

Huser, R., *The Crime of Abortion in Canon Law,* The Catholic University of America Canon Law Studies, n. 162, Washington, D.C.: The Catholic University of America Press, 1942.

Iorio, T., *Compendium Theologiae Moralis,* 5. ed., 2 vols., Neapoli: D'Auria, 1934-1935.

Jone, H., *Moral Theology,* 2. Eng. ed., tr. by Rev. Urban Adelman, Westminster, Md.: Newman, 1946.

Kehr, P., *Regesta Pontificum Romanorum. Italia Pontificia,* 8 vols. in 10, Berolini, 1906-1935.

Kelly, J.P., *Jurisdiction of the Confessor,* New York: Benziger, 1928.

Laymann, P., *Theologiae Moralis in V libros partitae liber V,* Venetiis, 1700.

Leech, G., *A Comparative Study of the Constitution* "Apostolicae Sedis" *and the* "Codex Iuris Canonici", The Catholic University of America Canon Law Studies, n. 15, Washington, D.C.: The Catholic University of America, 1922.

Liuzzi, F., *De delictis contra auctoritates ecclesiasticas,* Romae: Officum Libri Catholici, 1942.

Lugo, J., *Opera Omnia,* 8 vols. in 5, Venetiis, 1751.

Lyszczarczyk, V., *Compendium Privilegiorum Regularium praesertim Ordinis Fratrum Minorum,* Leopoli, 1906.

Mahoney, E., *Questions and Answers, The Sacraments,* London: Burns Oates & Washbourne, 1947.

Marc, C. - Gestermann, F., *Institutiones Morales Alphonsianae,* 17. ed., 2 vols., Lugduni: Vitte, 1922-1923.

Matulenas, R., *Communication—A Source of Privileges,* The Catholic University of America Canon Law Studies, n. 183, Washington, D. C.: The Catholic University of America Press, 1943.

McCormick, R., *Confessors of Religious,* The Catholic University of America Canon Law Studies, n. 33, Washington, D.C.: The Catholic University of America, 1926.

McGrath, J., *The Privilege of the Canon,* The Catholic University of America Canon Law Studies, n. 242, Washington, D.C.: The Catholic University of America Press, 1946.

Melo, A., *De Exemptione Regularium,* The Catholic University of America Canon Law Studies, n. 12, Washington, D.C.: The Catholic University of America, 1921.

Merkelbach, B., *Summa Theologia Moralis,* 3. ed., 3 vols., Parisiis: Desclée de Brouwer, 1938-1939.

Migne, J., *Patrologiae Cursus Completus. Series Latina,* 221 vols., Parisiis, 1878 - 1890.

Mocchegiani, P., *Iurisprudentia Ecclesiastica,* 3 vols., Quaracchi, 1904-1905.

Montalembert, C., *The Monks of the West,* 2 vols., Boston, ?

Moriarty, F., *The Extraordinary Absolution from Censures.* The Catholic University of America Canon Law Studies, n. 113, Washington, D. C.: The Catholic University of America, 1938.

Motry, H., *Diocesan Faculties according to the Code of Canon Law.* The Catholic University of America Canon Law Studies, n. 16, Washington, D.C.: The Catholic University of America, 1922.

National Catholic Almanac, The, Paterson, N. J.: St. Anthony's Guild, 1948.

Neuberger, N., *Canon 6 or the Relation of the Codex Iuris Canonici to Preceding Legislation.* The Catholic University of America Canon Law Studies, n. 44, Washington, D. C.: The Catholic University of America, 1927.

Noldin, H. - Schmitt, A., *Summa Theologica Moralis.* 3 vols.: Vols. I-II, 27. ed., 1940-1941; Vol. III, 26. ed., 1940, Oeniponte: Rauch.

O'Brien, J., *The Exemption of Religious in Church Law,* Milwaukee: Bruce, 1943.

Pejska, J., *Ius Canonicum Religiosorum,* 3. ed., Friburgi Brisgoviae: Herder, 1927.

Petrovits, J., *The New Church Law on Matrimony,* 2 - ed., Philadelphia: McVey 1926.

Piatus Montensis, *Praelectiones Iuris Regularis.* 3. ed., 2 vols., Tornaci: Casterman, 1906.

Poulet, C., *A History of the Catholic Church,* translated from the fourth French edition by Rev. Sydney A. Raemers, 2 vols., St. Louis: Herder, 1935-1936.

Pruemmer, D., *Manuale Iuris Ecclesiastici,* 2. ed., Friburgi Brisgoviae: Herder, 1920.

————*Manuale Theologiae Moralis,* 4. et 5. ed., 3 vols., Friburgi Brisgoviae: Herder, 1928.

Ramstein, M., *A Manual of Canon Law,* Hoboken, N.J.: Terminal Printing and Publishing Co., 1947.

Raus, J., *Institutiones Canonici*, Lugduni: Vitte, 1923.

Reiffenstuel, A., *Ius Canonicum Universum*, 5 vols. in 4, Monachii, 1702-1710.

Reilly, T., *The Visitation of Religious*, The Catholic University of America Canon Law Studies, n. 112, Washington, D.C.: The Catholic University of America, 1938.

Rodriguez, E., *Quaestiones Regulares et Canonicae*, 3 tomes in 1, Lugduni, 1613.

Roelker, E., *Principles of Privilege according to the Code of Canon Law*. The Catholic University of America Canon Law Studies, n. 35, Washington, D.C.: The Catholic University of America, 1926.

Schaefer, T., *De Religiosis*, 3. ed., Roma: S.A.L.E.R., 1940.

Schenk, F., *The Matrimonial Impediments of Mixed Religion and Disparity of Cult*, The Catholic University of America Canon Law Studies, n. 51, Washington, D.C.: The Catholic University of America, 1929.

Schmalzgrueber, F., *Ius Ecclesiasticum Universum*, 5 vols. in 12, Romae, 1843-1845.

Schroeder, H., *Disciplinary Decrees of the General Councils*, Text, Translation, and Commentary, St. Louis: Herder, 1937.

Shuhler, R.V., *Privileges of Regulars to Absolve and Dispense*. The Catholic University of America Canon Law Studies, n. 186, Washington, D.C.:

Sipos, S., *Enchiridion Iuris Canonici*, 3 ed., Pécs: Ex Typographia "Haladás R. T.," 1936.

Suarez, F., *Opera Omnia*, 26 vols. in 30, Parisiis, 1856-1861.

Thenhaven, B., *Nucleus Theologiae Canonico-Moralis*, Coesfeldiae, 1726.

Thomassinus, L., *Vetus et Nova Ecclesiae Disciplina circa Beneficia et Beneficiarios*, 10 vols., Moguntiae, 1787.

Ubach, J., *Theologia Moralis*, 2. ed., 2 vols., Bonis Auris: apud "Sociedad San Miguel", 1935.

Vascotti, C., *Institutiones Historiae Ecclesiasticae Novi Foederis*, 6. ed. recognita a Mathia Hiptmair, 2 vols., Vindobonae, 1895.

Vermeersch, A., *De Religiosis Institutis et Personis Supplementa et Monumenta*, 2 vols., Vol. I, 2. ed., 1907; Vol. II, 3. ed., 1904, Brugis.

Vermeersch, A. - Creusen, J., *Epitome Iuris Canonici*, 6. ed., 3 vols., Mechlinae-Romae: Dessain, 1937-1946.

Viva, D., *Cursus Theologico-moralis,* 3. ed., 2 vols., Beneventi, 1737.

Wernz, F. - Vidal, P., *Ius Canonicum,* 7 vols. in 8, Vol. II, 3. ed., 1943, Romae: apud Aedes Universitatis Gregorianae, 1925-1943.

Wouters, L., *Manuale Theologiae Moralis,* 2 vols., Brugis: Beyaert, 1932-1933.

Woywod, S., *A Practical Commentary on the Code of Canon Law,* revised ed., 2 vols., New York: Wagner, 1944.

Zeiger, I., *Historia Iuris Canonici,* 2 vols., Romae: apud Aedes Universitatis Gregorianae, 1939-1840.

Articles

Anonymous, "Absolutio a Censuris Papalibus Ordinariis Reservatis"—*ER* LXVII (1922), 518-522.

——— "Cases Reserved by Code and by Ordinary"—*ER,* LXXXIV (1931), 190-192.

——— "Reply to Father Vitali's Objections"—*ER,* LXXXV (1931), 75-82.

——— "Reply to Fr. Vitali's Renewed Objections"—*ER,* LXXXVI (1932), 297-305.

Callebaut, A., "Les Provinciaux de la Province de France au XIIIe siécle Notes, documents et études."—*Archivum Franciscanum Historicum,* X (1917), 289-356.

Connell, F., "The Place for a Woman's Confession"—*The American Ecclesiastical Review,* CXVIII (1948), 62-63.

"De confessione sacramentali in ordine nostro"—*Acta Ordinis Fratrum Minorum,* LXI (1942), 45-50.

Goyeneche, S., "Consultationes"—*CpR,* VII (1926), 40.

Gratien, P., "Ordres mendicants et clergé sécullier a la fin du XIIIe siecle."—*Etudes franciscaines,* XXXVI (1924), 499-518.

Larraona, A., "Commentarium"—*CpR,* X (1929), 248-259, 355-367.

Vitali, I., "De Absolutione a Censuris Papalibus Ordinariis Reservatis deque Regularium Privilegio ab iisdem Absolvendi"—*HPR,* XXIII (1923), 1284-1285.

———— "De Mixtis Reservationibus"—*ER*, LXXXI (1924), 517-520.

———— "Adhuc de Mixtis Reservationibus"—*ER*, LXXXV (1931), 73-75.

———— "Utrum Locorum Ordinarii Valeant Suspendere Privilegium Regularium 'Absolvendi a Casibus Papalibus Ordinariis Reservatis' per accidens et via exceptionis"—*ER*, LXXXVI (1932), 292-296.

———— "De reservationibus pontificiis a iure reservatis ordinario deque Regularium privilegio ab iisdem absolvendi"—*CpR*, XIV (1933). 287-294, 363-375, 436-447.

———— "Circa casus a iure reservatos necnon circa privilegium regularium absolvendi a casibus papalibus ordinariis reservatis"—*CpRM*, XVI (1935), 164-175.

Voltas, P., "De reservatione episcopali quoad regulares"—*CpR*, III (1922), 69-77.

Woywod, S., "Reservation by Local Ordinaries of Sins Punished with a Censure in the Common Law"—*HPR*, XXXI (1931), 869-870.

Periodicals

American Ecclesiastical Review, The, Vols. I-XXXII, Philadelphia, 1895-1905; from 1905: *The Ecclesiastical Review,* Vols. XXXIII-CIX, Philadelphia, 1905-1943; from 1944: *The American Ecclesiastical Review,* Washington, D. C., Vol. CX, 1944—

Archivum Franciscanum Historicum, Quaracchi, 1907—

Commentarium pro Religiosis, Romae, 1920—; ab anno 1935: *Commentarium pro Religiosis et Missionariis,*

Etudes franciscaines, Paris, 1899—

Homiletic and Pastoral Review, The, New York, 1900—

Abbreviations

AAS—*Acta Apostolicae Sedis.*

Bull. Francisc.—*Bullarium Franciscanum*, editum studio et labore Joannis Hyacinthi Sbaraleae.

Bull. Rom. Taur.—*Bullarum Diplomatum et Privilegiorum Sanctorum Romanorum Pontificum Taurinensis editio.*

CpR[M]—*Commentarium pro Religiosis* [*et Missionariis*]

Decr.—decretum.

ER—*The Ecclesiastical Review.*

Fontes—*Codicis Iuris Canonici Fontes cura . . . Gasparri editi.*

HPR—*The Homiletic and Pastoral Review.*

Instr.—instructio.

JE—Jaffé, *Regesta Pontificum Romanorum* (edited by Ewald).

JK—Jaffé, *Regesta Pontificum Romanorum* (edited by Kaltenbrunner).

JL—Jaffé, *Regesta Pontificum Romanorum* (edited by Loewenfeld).

S. C. de Religiosis—Sacra Congregatio de Religiosis.

S. C. Ep. et Reg.—Sacra Congregatio Episcoporum et Regularium.

S. C. S. Off.—Suprema Congregatio Sancti Officii.

INDEX

—o—

BIOGRAPHICAL NOTE

Marcellus Anthony McCartney was born in Townhead, Glasgow, Scotland, on December 8, 1913. His primary education was completed in America in January, 1927. He entered St. Joseph's Seraphic Seminary, Callicoon, N.Y., in September, 1931, and the Franciscan Novitiate at Paterson, N.J., in August, 1938. After simple profession in August, 1939, he pursued his philosophical studies. receiving the Degree of Bachelor of Arts from St. Bonaventure College, Allegany, N.Y., in June 1941. He studied theology at Holy Name College, Washington, D.C., and was ordained to the priesthood on June 11, 1944. He completed his fourth year of theology in 1945, and received in the same year the Degree of Master of Arts from St. Bonaventure College. After enrolling in the School of Canon Law at the Catholic University of America in October, 1945, he received the Baccalaureate Degree in Canon Law in June, 1946, and the Licentiate Degree in Canon Law in June, 1947.

CANON LAW STUDIES *

1. FRERIKS, REV. CELESTINE A., C.PP.S., J.C.D., Religious Congregations in Their External Relations, 121 pp., 1916.
2. GALLIHER, REV. DANIEL M., O.P., J.C.D., Canonical Elections, 117 pp., 1917.
3. BORKOWSKI, REV. AURELIUS L., O.F.M., J.C.D., De Confraternitatibus Ecclesiasticis, 136 pp., 1918.
4. CASTILLO, REV. CAYO, J.C.D., Disertacion Historico-Canonica sobre la Potestad del Cabildo en Sede Vacante o Impedida del Vicario Capitular, 99 pp., 1919 (1918).
5. KUBELBECK, REV. WILLIAM J., *S.T.B., J.C.D., The Sacred Penitentiaria* and Its Relation to Faculties of Ordinaries and Priests, 129 pp., 1918.
6. PETROVITS, REV. JOSEPH J. C., S.T.D., J.C.D., The New Church Law on Matrimony, X-461 pp., 1919.
7. HICKEY, REV. JOHN J., S.T.B., J.C.D., Irregularities and Simple Impediments in the New Code of Canon Law, 100 pp., 1920.
8. KLEKOTKA, REV. PETER J., S.T.B., J.C.D., Diocesan Consultors, 179 pp., 1920.
9. WANENMACHER, REV. FRANCIS, *J.C.D., The Evidence in Ecclesi*astical Procedure Affecting the Marriage Bond, 1920 (Printed 1935).
10. GOLDEN, REV. HENRY FRANCIS, *J.C.D., Parochial Benefices in the* New Code, IV-119 pp., 1921 (Printed 1925).
11. KOUDELKA, REV. CHARLES J., J.C.D., Pastors, Their Rights and Duties According to the New Code of Canon Law, 211 pp., 1921.
12. MELO, REV. ANTONIUS, O.F.M., J.C.D., De Exemptione Regularium, X-188 pp., 1921.
13. SCHAFF, REV. VALENTINE THEODORE, O.F.M., S.T.B., J.C.D., The Cloister, X-180 pp., 1921.
14. BURKE, REV. THOMAS JOSEPH, S.T.D., J.C.D., Competence in Ecclesiastical Tribunals, IV-117 pp., 1922.
15. LEECH, REV. GEORGE LEO, J.C.D., A Comparative Study of the Constitution "Apostolicae Sedis" and the "Codex Juris Canonici," 179 pp., 1922.

* All published numbers are available from the Catholic University of America Press, 621 Michigan Avenue, N.E., Washington 17, D.C., except the following : Numbers 1-114 inclusive, and numbers 116, 118, 120, 122, 123, 136, 162, and 198.

16. MOTRY, REV. HUBERT LOUIS., S.T.D., J.C.D., Diocesan Faculties According to the Code of Canon Law, II-167 pp., 1922.

17. MURPHY, REV. GEORGE LAWRENCE, J.C.D., Delinquencies and Penalties in the Administratian and the Reception of the Sacraments, IV-121 pp., 1923.

18. O'REILLY, REV. JOHN ANTHONY, S.T.B., J.C.D., Ecclesiastical Sepulture in the New Code of Canon Law, II-129 pp., 1923.

19. MICHALICKA, REV. WENCESLAUS CYRILL, O.S.B., J.C.D., Judicial Procedure in Dismissal of Clerical Exempt Religious, 107 pp., 1923.

20. DARGIN, REV. EDWARD VINCENT, S.T.B., J.C.D., Reserved Cases According to the Code of Canon Law, IV-103 pp., 1924.

21. GODFREY, REV. JOHN A., S.T.B., J.C.D., The Right of Patronage According to the Code of Canon Law, 153 pp., 1924.

22. HAGEDORN, REV. FRANCIS EDWARD, J.C.D., General Legislation on Indulgences, II-154 pp., 1924.

23. KING, REV. JAMES IGNATIUS, J.C.D., The Administration of the Sacraments to Dying Non-Catholics, V-141 pp., 1924.

24. WINSLOW, REV. FRANCIS JOSEPH, M.M., J.C.D., Vicars and Prefects Apostolic, IV-149 pp., 1924.

25. CORREA, REV. JOSE SERVELION, S.T.L., J.C.D., La Potestad Legislativa de la Iglesia Catolica, IV-127 pp., 1925.

26. DUGAN, REV. HENRY FRANCIS, A.M., J.C.D., The Judiciary Department of the Diocesan Curia, 87, pp., 1925.

27. KELLER, REV. CHARLES FREDERICK, S.T.B., J.C.D., Mass Stipends, 167 pp., 125.

28. PASCHANG, REV. JOHN LINUS, J.C.D., The Sacraments According to the Code of Canon Law, 129 pp., 1925.

29. PIONTEK, REV. CYRILLUS, O.F.M., S.T.B., J.C.D., De Indulto Exclaustrationis necnon Sæcularizationis, XIII-289 pp., 1925.

30. KEARNEY, REV. RICHARD JOSEPH, S.T.B., J.C.D., Sponsors at Baptism According to the Code of Canon Law, IV-127 pp., 1925.

31. BARTLETT, REV. CHESTER JOSEPH, A.M., LL.B., J.C.D., The Tenure of Parochial Property in the United States of America, V-108 pp., 1926.

32. KILKER, REV. ADRIAN JEROME, J.C.D., Extreme Unction, V-425 pp., 1926.

33. MCCORMICK, REV. ROBERT EMMETT, J.C.D., Confessors of Religious, VIII-266 pp., 1926.

34. MILLER, REV. NEWTON THOMAS, J.C.D., Founded Masses According to the Code of Canon Law, VII-93 pp., 1926.

35. ROELKER, REV. EDWARD G., S.T.D., J.C.D., Principles of Privilege According to the Code of Canon Law, XI-166 pp., 1926.

36. BAKALARCZYK, REV. RICHARDUS, M.I.C., J.U.D., De Novitiatu, VIII-208 pp., 1927.

37. PIZZUTI, REV. LAWRENCE, O.F.M., J.U.L., De Parochis Religiosis, 1927. (Not Printed.)

38. BLILEY, REV. NICHOLAS MARTIN, O.S.B., J.C.D., Altars According to the Code of Canon Law, XIX-132 pp., 1927.

38. BROWN, MR. BRENDAN FRANCIS, A.B., LL.M., J.U.D., The Canonical Juristic Personality with Special Reference to its Status in the United States of America, V-212 pp., 1927.

40. CAVANAUGH, REV. WILLIAM THOMAS, C.P., J.U.D., The Reservation of the Blessed Sacrament, VIII-101 pp., 1927.

41. DOHENY, REV. WILLIAM J., C.S.C., A.B., J.U.D., Church Property Modes of Acquisition, X-118 pp., 1927.

42. FELDHAUS, REV. ALOYSIUS H., C.PP.S., J.C.D., Oratories, IX-141 pp., 1927.

43. KELLY, REV. JAMES PATRICK, A.B., J.C.D., The Jurisdiction of the Simple Confessor, X-208 pp., 1927.

44. NEUBERGER, REV. NICHOLAS J., J.C.D., Canon 6 or the Relation of the Codex Juris Canonici to the Preceding Legislation, V-95 pp., 1927.

45. O'KEEFE, REV. GERALD MICHAEL, J.C.D., Matrimonial Dispensations, Powers of Bishops, Priests, and Confessors, VIII-232 pp., 1927.

46. QUIGLEY, REV. JOSEPH A. M., A.B., J.C.D. Condemned Societies, 139 pp., 1927.

47. ZAPLOTNIK, REV. JOHANNES LEO, J.C.D., De Vicariis Foraneis, X-142 pp., 1927.

48. DUSKIE, REV. JOHN ALOYSIUS, A.B., J.C.D., The Canonical Status of The Orientals in the United States, VIII-196 pp., 1928.

49. HYLAND, REV. FRANCIS EDWARD, J.C.D., Excommunication, Its Nature, Historical Development and Effects, VII-181 pp., 1928.

50. REINMANN, REV. GERALD JOSEPH, O.M.C., J.C.D., The Third Order Secular of Saint Francis, 201 pp., 1928.

51. SCHENK, REV. FRANCIS J., J.C.D., The Matrimonial Impediments of Mixed Religion and Disparity of Cult, XVI-318 pp., 1929.

52. COADY, REV. JOHN JOSEPH, S.T.D., J.U.D., A.M., The Appointment of Pastors, VIII-150 pp., 1929.

53. KAY, REV. THOMAS HENRY, J.C.D., Competence in Matrimonial Procedure, VIII-164 pp., 1929.

54. TURNER, REV. SIDNEY JOSEPH, C.P., J.U.D., The Vow of Poverty, XLIX-217 pp., 1929.
55. KEARNEY, REV. RAYMOND A., A.B., S.T.D., J.C.D., The Principles of Delegation, VII-149 pp., 1929.
56. CONRAN, REV. EDWARD JAMES, A.B., J.C.D., The Interdict, V-163 pp., 1930.
57. O'NEILL, REV. WILLAIM H., J.C.D., Papal Rescripts of Favor, VII-218 pp., 1930.
58. BASTNAGEL, REV. CLEMENT VINCENT, J.U.D., The Appointment of Parochial Adjutants and Assistants, XV-257 pp., 1930.
59. FERRRY, REV. WILLIAM A., A.B., J.C.D., Stole Fees, V-136 pp., 1930.
60. COSTELLO, REV. JOHN MICHAEL, A.B., J.C.D., Domicile and Quasi-Domicile, VII-201 pp., 1930.
61. KREMER, REV. MICHAEL NICHOLAS, A.B., S.T.B., J.C.D., Church Support in the United States, VI-136 pp., 1930.
62. ANGULO, REV. LIUS, C.M., J.C.D., Legislation de la Iglesia sobre la intencion en la application de la Santa Misa, VII-104 pp., 1931.
63. FREY, REV. WOLFGANG NORBERT, O.S.B., A.B., J.C.D., The Act of Religious Profession, VIII-174 pp. 1931.
64. ROBERTS, REV. JAMES BRENDAN, A.B., J.C.D., The Banns of Marriage XIV-140 pp., 1931.
65. RYDER, REV. RAYMOND ALOYSIUS, A.B., J.C.D., Simony, IX-151 pp., 1931.
66. CAMPAGNA, REV. ANGELO, PHD., J.U.D., Il Vicario Generale del Vescovo, VII-205 pp., 1931.
67. COX, REV. JOSEPH GODFREY, A.B., J.C.D., The Administration of Seminaries, VI-124 pp., 1931.
68. GREGORY, REV. DONALD J., J.U.D., The Pauline Privilege, XV-165 pp., 1931.
69. DONOHUE, REV. JOHN F., J.C.D., The Impediment of Crime, VII-110 pp., 1931.
70. DOOLEY, REV. EUGENE A., O.M.I., J.C.D., Church Law on Sacred Relics, IX-143 pp., 1931.
71. ORTH, REV. CLEMENT RAYMOND, O.M.C., J.C.D., The Approbation of Religious Institutes, 171 pp., 1931.
72. PERNICONE, REV. JOSEPH M., A.B., J.C.D., The Ecclesiastical Prohibition of Books, XII-267 pp., 1932.
73. CLINTON, REV. CONNELL, A.B., J.C.D., The Paschal Precept, IX-108 pp., 1932.

74. DONNELLY, REV. FRANCIS B., A.M., S.T.L., J.C.D., The Diocesan Synod, VIII-125 pp., 1932.
75. TORRENTE, REV. CAMILO, C.M.F., J.C.D., Las Procesiones Sagradas, V-145 pp., 1932.
76. MURPHY, REV. EDWIN J., C.P.P.S., J.C.D., Suspension Ex Informata Conscientia, XI-122 pp., 1932.
77. MACKENZIE, REV. ERIC F., A.M., S.T.L., J.C.D., The Delict of Heresy in its Commission, Penalization, Absolution, VII-124 pp., 1932.
78. LYONS, REV. AVITUS E., S.T.B., J.C.D., The Collegiate Tribunal of First Instance, XI-147 pp., 1932.
79. CONNOLLY, REV. THOMAS A., J.C.D., Appeals, XI-195 pp., 1932.
80. SANGMEISTER, REV. JOSEPH V., A.B., J.C.D., Force and Fear as Precluding Matrimonial Consent, V-211 pp., 1932.
81. JAEGER, REV. LEO A., A.B., J.C.D., The Administration of Vacant and Quasi-Vacant Episcopal Sees in the United States, IX-299 pp., 1932.
82. RIMLINGER, REV. HERBERT T., J.C.D., Error Invalidating Matrimonial Consent, VII-79 pp., 1932.
83. BARRETT, REV. JOHN D. M., S.S., J.C.D., A Comparative Study of the Councils of Baltimore and the Code of Canon Law, X-223 pp., 1932.
84. CARBERRY, REV. JOHN J., PH.D., S.T.D., J.C.D., The Juridical Form of Marriage, X-177 pp., 1934.
85. DOLAN, REV. JOHN L., A.B., J.C.D., The Defensor Vinculi, XII-157 pp., 1934.
86. HANNAN, REV. JEROME D., A.M., S.T.D., LL.B., J.C,D,, The Canon Law of Wills, IX-517 pp., 1934.
87. LEMIEUX, REV. DELISE A., A.M., J.C.D., The Sentence in Ecclesiastical Procedure, IX-131 pp., 1934.
88. O'ROURKE, REV. JAMES J., A.B., J.C.D., Parish Registers, VII-109 pp., 1934.
89. TIMLIN, REV. BARTHOLOMEW, O.F.M., A.M., J.C.D., Conditional Matrimonial Consent, X-381 pp., 1934.
90. WAHL, REV. FRANCIS X., A.B., J.C.D., The Matrimonial Impediments of Consanguinity and Affinity, VI-125 pp., 1934.
91. WHITE, REV. ROBERT J., A.B., LL.B., S.T.B., J.C.D., Canonical Ante-Nuptial Promises and the Civil Law, VI-152 pp., 1934.
92. HERRARA, REV. ANTONIO PARRA, O.C.D., J.C.D., Legislacion Ecclesiastica sobra el Ayuno y la Abstinencia, XI-191 pp., 1935.

93. KENNEDY, REV. EDWIN J., J.C.D., The Special Matrimonial Process in Cases of Evident Nullity, X-165 pp., 1935.

94. MANNING, REV. JOHN J., A.B., J.C.D., Presumption of Law in Matrimonial Procedure, XI-111 pp., 1935.

95. MOEDER, REV. JOHN M., J.C.D., The Proper Bishop for Ordination and Dimissorial Letters, VII-135 pp., 1935.

96. O'MARA, REV. WILLIAM A., A.B., J.C.D., Canonical Causes for Matrimonial Dispensations, IX-155 pp., 1935.

97. REILLY, REV. PETER, J.C.D., Residence of Pastors, IX-81 pp., 1935.

98. SMITH, REV. MARINER T., O.P., S.T.LR., J.C.D., The Penal Law for Religious, VIII-169 pp., 1935.

99. WHALEN, REV. DONALD W., A.M., J.C.D., The Value of Testimonial Evidence in Matrimonial Procedure, XIII-297 pp., 1935.

100. CLEARY, REV. JOSEPH F., J.C.D., Canonical Limitations on the Alienation of Church Property, VIII-141 pp., 1936.

101. GLYNN, REV. JOHN C., J.C.D., The Promoter of Justice, XX-337 pp., 1936.

102. BRENNAN, REV. JAMES H., S.S., M.A., S.T.B., J.C.D., The Simple Convalidation of Marriage, VI-135 pp., 1937.

103. BRUNINI, REV. JOSEPH BERNARD, J.C.D., The Clerical Obligations of Canons 139 and 142, X-121 pp., 1937.

104. CONNOR, REV. MAURICE, A.B., J.C.D., The Administrative Removal of Pastors, VIII-159 pp., 1937.

105. GUILFOYLE, REV. MERLIN JOSEPH, J.C.D., Custom, XI-144 pp., 1937.

106. HUGHES, REV. JAMES AUSTIN, A.B., A.M., J.C.D., Witnesses in Criminal Trials of Clerics, IX-140 pp., 1937.

107. JANSEN, REV. RAYMOND J., A.B., S.T.L., J.C.D., Canonical Provisions for Catechetical Instruction, VII-153 pp., 1937.

108. KEALY, REV. JOHN JAMES, A.B., J.C.D., The Introductory Libellus in Church Court Procedure, XI-121 pp., 1937.

109. MCMANUS, REV. JAMES EDWARD, C.S.S.R., J.C.D., The Administration of Temporal Goods in Religious Institutes, XVI-196 pp., 1937.

110. MORIARTY, REV. EUGENE JAMES, J.C.D., Oaths in Ecclesiastical Courts, X-115 pp., 1937.

111. RAINER, REV. ELIGIUS GEORGE, C.SS.R., J.C.D., Suspension of Clerics, XVII-249 pp., 1937.

112. REILLY, REV. THOMAS F., C.SS.R., J.C.D., Visitation of Religious, VI-195 pp., 1938.

113. MORIARTY, REV. FRANCIS E., C.SS.R., J.C.D., The Extraordinary Absolution from Censures, XV-334 pp., 1938.

114. CONNOLLY, REV. NICHOLAS P., J.C.D., The Canonical Erection of Parishes, X-132 pp., 1938.

115. DONOVAN, REV. JAMES JOSEPH, J.C.D., The Pastor's Obligation in Prenuptial Investigation, XII-322 pp., 1938.

116. HARRIGAN, REV. ROBERT J., M.A., S.T.B., J.C.D., The Radical Sanation of Invalid Marriages, VIII-208 pp., 1938.

117. BOFFA, REV. CONRAD HUMBERT, J.C.D., Canonical Provisions for Catholic Schools, VII-211 pp., 1939.

118. PARSONS, REV. ANSCAR JOHN, O.M.CAP., J.C.D., Canonical Elections, XII-236 pp., 1939.

119. REILLY, REV. EDWARD MICHAEL, A.B., J.C.D., The General Norms of Dispensation, XII-156 pp., 1939.

120. RYAN, REV. GERALD ALOYSIUS, A.B., J.C.D., Principles of Episcopal Jurisdiction, XII-172 pp., 1939.

121. BURTON, REV. FRANCIS JAMES, C.S.C., A.B., J.C.D., A Commentary on Canon 1125, X-222 pp., 1940.

122. MIASKIEWICZ, REV. FRANCIS SIGISMUND, J.C.D., Supplied Jurisdiction According to Canon 209, XII-340 pp., 1940.

123. RICE, REV. PARTICK WILLIAM, A.B., J.C.D., Proof of Death in Prenuptial Investigation, VIII-156 pp., 1940.

124. ANGLIN, REV. THOMAS FRANCIS, M.S., J.C.D., The Eucharistic Fast, VIII-183 pp., 1941.

125. COLEMAN, REV. JOHN JEROME, J.C.D., The Minister of Confirmation, VI-153 pp., 1941.

126. DOWNS, REV. JOSEPH EMMANUEL, A.B., J.C.D., The Concept of Clerical Immunity, XI-163 pp., 1941.

127. ESSWEIN, REV. ANTHONY ALBERT, J.C.D., Extrajudicial Penal Powers of Ecclesiastical Superiors, X-144 pp., 1941.

128. FARRELL, REV. BENJAMIN FRANCIS, M.A., S.T.L., J.C.D., The Rights and Duties of the Local Ordinary Regarding Congregations of Women Religious of Pontifical Approval, V-195 pp., 1941.

129. FEENEY, REV. THOMAS JOHN, A.B., S.T.L., J.C.D., Restitutio in Integrum, VI-169 pp., 1941.

130. FINDLAY, REV. STEPHEN WILLIAM, O.S.B., A.B., J.C.D., Canonical Norms Governing the Deposition and Degradation of Clerics, XVII-279 pp., 1941.

131 GOODWINE, REV. JOHN, A.B., S.T.L., J.C.D., The Right of the Church to Acquire Property, VIII-119 pp., 1941.

132. HESTON, REV. EDWARD LOUIS, C.S.C., PH.D., S.T.D., J.C.D., The Alienation of Church Property in the United States, XII-222 pp., 1941.

133. HOGAN, REV. JAMES JOHN, A.B., S.T.L., J.C.D., Judicial Advocates and Procurators, XIII-200 pp., 1941.

134. KEALY, REV. THOMAS M., A.B., LITT.B., J.C.D., Dowry of Women Religious, IX-152 pp., 1941.

135. KEENE, REV. MICHAEL JAMES, O.S.B., J.C.D., Religious Ordinaries and Canon 198, V-164 pp., 1942.

136. KERIN, REV. CHARLES A., S.S., M.A., S.T.B., J.C.D., The Privation of Christian Burial, XVI-279 pp., 1941.

137. LOUIS, REV. WILLIAM FRANCIS, M.A., J.C.D., Diocesan Archives, X-101 pp., 1941.

138. MCDEVITT, REV. GILBERT JOSEPH, A.B., J.C.D., Legitimacy and Legitimation, X-247 pp., 1941.

139. MCDONOUGH, REV. THOMAS JOSEPH, A.B., J.C.D., Apostolic Administrators, X-217 pp., 1941.

140. MEIER, REV. CARL ANTHONY, A.B., J.C.D., Penal Administrative Procedure Against Negligent Pastors, XI-240 pp., 1941.

141. SCHMIDT, REV. JOHN ROGG, A.B., J.C.D., The Principles of Authentic Interpretation in Canon 17 of the Code of Canon Law, XII-331 pp., 1941.

142. SLAFKOSKY, REV. ANDREW LEONARD, *A.B., J.C.D., The Canonical* Episcopal Visitations of the Diocese, X-197 pp., 1941.

143. SWOBODA, REV. INNOCENT ROBERT, O.F.M., J.C.D., Ignorance in Relation to the Imputability of Delicts, IX-271 pp., 1941.

144. DUBE, REV. ARTHUR JOSEPH, A.B., J.C.D., The General Principles for the Reckoning of Time in Canon Law, VIII-299 pp., 1941.

145. MCBRIDE, REV. JAMES T., A.B., J.C.D., Incardination and Excardination of Seculars, XX-585 pp., 1941.

146. KROL, REV. JOHN T., J.C.D., The Defendant in Ecclesiastical Trials, XII-207 pp., 1942.

147. COMYNS, REV. JOSEPH J., C.S.S.R., A.B., J.C.D., Papal and Episcopal Administration of Church Property, XIV-155 pp., 1942.

148. Barry, Rev. Garrett Francis, O.M.I., J.C.D., Violation of the Cloister, XII-260 pp., 1942.

149. Bolduc, Rev. Gatien, C.S.V., A.B., S.T.L., J.C.D., Les Etudes dans les Religions Cléricales, VIII-155 pp., 1942.

150. Boyle, Rev. David John, M.A., J.C.D., The Juridic Effects of Moral Certitude on Pre-Nuptial Guarantees, XII-188 pp., 1942.

151. Canavan, Rev. Walter Joseph, M.A., Litt.D., J.C.D., The Profession of Faith, XII-143 pp., 1942.

152. Desrochers, Rev. Bruno, A.B., P .L., S.T.B., J.C.D., Le Premier Concile Plénier de Québec et le Code de Droit Canonique, XIV-186 pp., 1942.

153.Dillon, Rev. Robert Edward, A.B., J.C.D., Common Law Marriage, X-148 pp., 1942.

154. Dodwell, Rev. Edward John, PhD., S.T.B., J.C.D., The Time and Place for the Celebration of Marriage, X-156 pp., 1942.

155. Donnellan, Rev. Thomas Andrew, A.B., J.C.D., The Obligation of the Missa pro Populo, VII-131 pp., 1942.

156. Eltz, Rev. Louis Anthony, A.B., J.C.D., Coöperation in Crime, XII-208 pp., 1942.

157. Gass, Rev. Sylvester Francis, M.A., J.C.D., Ecclesiastical Pensions, XI-206 pp., 1942.

158. Guiniven, Rev. John Joseph, C.SS.R., J.C.D., The Precept of Hearing Mass, XIV-188 pp., 1942.

159. Gulczynski, Rev. John Theophilus, J.C.D., The Desecration and Violation of Churches, X-126 pp., 1942.

160. Hammill, Rev. John Leo, M.A., J.C.D., The Obligations of the Traveler According to Canon 14, VIII-204 pp., 1942.

161. Haydt, Rev. John Joseph, A.B., J.C.D., Reserved Benefices, XI-148 pp., 1942.

162. Huser, Rev. Roger John, O.F.M., A.B., J.C.D., The Crime of Abortion in Canon Law, XII-187 pp., 1942.

163. Kearney, Rev. Francis Patrick, A.B., S.T.L., J.C.D., The Principles of Canon 1127, X-162 pp., 1942.

164. Linahen, Rev. Leo James, S.T.L., J.C.D., De Absolutione Complicis in Peccato Turpi, 114 pp., 1942.

165. McCloskey, Rev. Joseph Aloysius, A.B., J.C.D., The Subject of Ecclesiastical Law According to Canon 12, XVII-246 pp., 1942.

166. O'Neill, Rev. Francis Joseph, C.SS.R., J.C.D., The Dismissal of Religious in Temporary Vows, XIII-220 pp., 1942.

167. PRINCE, REV. JOHN EDWARD, A.B., S.T.D. J.C.D., The Diocesan Chancellor, X-136 pp., 1942.

168. RIESNER, REV. ALBERT JOSEPH, C.SS.R., J.C.D., Apostates and Fugitives from Religious Institutes, IX-168 pp., 1942.

169. STENGER, REV. JOSEPH BERNARD, J.C.D., The Mortgaging of Church Property, 186 pp., 1942.

170. WALDRON, REV. JOSEPH FRANCIS, A.B., J.C.D., The Minister of Baptism, XII-197 pp., 1942.

171. WILLET, REV. ROBERT ALBERT, J.C.D., The Probative Value of Documents in Ecclesiastical Trials, X-124 pp., 1942.

172. WOEBER, REV. EDWARD MARTIN, M.A., J.C.D., The Interpellations, XII-161 pp., 1942.

173. BENKO, REV. MATTHEW ALOYSIUS, O.S.B., M.A., J.C.D., The Abbot *Nullius*, XVI-148 pp., 1943.

174. CHRIST, REV. JOSEPH JAMES, M.A., S.T.L., J.C.D., Dispensation from Vindicative Penalties, XIII-285 pp., 1943.

175. CLANCY, REV. PATRICK M. J., O.P., A.B., S.T.LR., J.C.D., The Local Religious Superior, X-229 pp, 1943.

176. CLARKE, REV. THOMAS JAMES, J.C.D., Parish Societies, XII-147 pp., 1943.

177. CONNOLLY, REV. JOHN PATRICK, S.T.L., J.C.D., Synodal Examiners, and Parish Priest Consultors, X-223 pp., 1943.

178. DRUMM, REV. WILLIAM MARTIN, A.B., J.C.D., Hospital Chaplains, XII-175 pp., 1943.

179. FLANAGAN,, REV. BERNARD JOSEPH, A.B., S.T.L., J.C.D., The Canonical Erection of Religious Houses, X-147 pp., 1943.

180. KELLEHER, REV. STEPHEN JOSEPH, A.B., S.T.B., J.C.D., Discussions with Non-Catholics: Canonical Legislation, X-93 pp., 1943.

181. LEWIS, REV. GORDIAN, C.P., J.C.D., Chapters in Religious Institutes, XII-169 pp., 1943.

182. MARX, REV. ADOLPH, J.C.D., The Declaration of Nullity of Marriages Contracted Outside the Church, X-151 pp., 1943.

183. MATULENAS, REV. RAYMOND ANTHONY, O.S.B., A.B., J.C.D., Communication, a Source of Privileges, XII-225 pp., 1943.

184. O'LEARY, REV. CHARLES GERARD, C.S.S.R., J.C.D., Religious Dismissed After Perpelual Profession, X-213 pp., 1943.

185. POWER, REV. CORNELIUS MICHAEL, J.C.D., The Blessing of Cemeteries, XII-231 pp., 1943.

186. SHUHLER, REV. RALPH VINCENT, O.S.A., J.C.D., Privileges of Religious to Absolve and Dispense, XII-195 pp., 1943.

187. ZIOLKOWSKI, REV. THADDEUS STANISLAUS, A.B., J.C.D., The Consecration and Blessing of Churches, XII-151 pp., 1943.

188. HENEGHAN, REV. JOHN JOSEPH, S.T.D., J.C.D., The Marriagee of Unworthy Catholics: Canons 1065 and 1066, XVI-213 pp., 1944.

189. CARROLL, REV. COLEMAN FRANCIS, M.A., S.T.L., J.C.L., Charitable Institutions.

190. CIESLUK, REV. JOSEPH EDWARD, PH.B., S.T.L., J.C.D., National Parishes in the United States, VI-178 pp., 1944.

191. COBURN, REV. VINCENT PAUL, A.B., J.C.D., Marriages of Conscience, XII-172 pp., 1944.

192. CONNORS, REV. CHARLES PAUL, C.S.S.P., A.B., J.C.D., Extra Judical Procurators in the Code of Canon Law, X-94 pp., 1944.

193. COYLE, REV. PAUL RAYMOND, A.B., J.C.D., Judicial Exceptions, IX-142 pp., 1944.

194. FAIR, REV. BARTHOLOMEW FRANCIS, A.B., S.T.L., J.C.D., The Impediment of Abduction, XII-122 pp., 1944.

195. GALLAGHER, REV. THOMAS RAPHAEL, O.P., A.B., S.T.LR., J.C.D., The Examination of the Qualities of the Ordinand, X-166 pp., 1944.

196. GANNON, REV. JOHN MARK, S.T.L., J.C.D., The Interstices Required for the Promotion to Orders, VII-100 pp., 1944.

197. GOLDSMITH, REV. J. WILLIAM, B.C.S., S.T.L., J.C.D., The Competence of Church and State Over Marriage — Disputed Points, X-128 pp., 1944.

198. GOODWINE, REV. JOSEPH GERARD, A.B., S.T.B., J.C.D., The Reception of Converts, XIV-326 pp., 1944.

199. KOWALSKI, REV. ROMUALD EUGENE, O.F.M., A.B., J.C.D., Sustenance of Religious Houses of Regulars, X-174 pp., 1944.

200. MCCOY, REV. ALAN EDWARD, O.F.M., J.C.D., Force and Fear in Relation to Delictual Imputability and Penal Responsibility, XII-160 pp., 1944.

201. MCDEVITT, REV. VINCENT JOHN, PH.B., S.T.L., J.C.L., Perjury.

202. MARTIN, REV. THOMAS OWEN, PH.D., S.T.D., J.C.D., Adverse Possession, Prescription and Limitation of Actions: The Canonical "Præscriptio," XX-208 pp., 1944.

203. MIKLOSOVIC, REV. PAUL JOHN, A.B., J.C.L., Attempted Marriages and Their Consequent Juridic Effects.

204. MUNDY, REV. THOMAS MAURICE, A.B., S.T.L., J.C.D., The Union of Parishes, X-164 pp., 1944.

205. O'DEA, REV. JOHN COYLE, A.B., J.C.D., The Matrimonial Impediment of Nonage, VIII-126 pp., 1944.

206. OLALIA, REV. ALEXANDER AYSON, S.T.L., J.C.D., A Comparative Study of the Christian Constitution of States and the Constitution of the Philippine Commonwealth, XII-136 pp., 1944.

207. POISSON, REV. PIERRE-MARIE, C.S.C., A.B., PH.L., TH.L., J.C.L., Droits Patrimoniaux des Maisons et des Eglises Religieuses.

208. STADALNIKAS, REV. CASIMIR JOSEPH, M.I.C., J.C.D., Reservation of Censures, X-141 pp., 1944.

209. SULLIVAN, REV. EUGENE HENRY, S.T.L., J.C.D., Proof of the Reception of the Sacraments, X-165 pp., 1944.

210. VAUGHAN, REV. WILLIAM EDWARD, J.C.D., Constitutions for Diocesan Courts, X-210 pp., 1944.

211. PARO, REV. GINO, S.T.D., J.C.L., The Right of Apostolic Delegation.

212. BALZER, REV. RALPH FRANCIS, C.P., J.C.D., The Computation of Time in a Canonical Novitiate, X-227 pp., 1945.

213. DOUGHERTY, REV. JOHN WHELAN, A.B., S.T.L., J.C.D., De Inquisitione Speciali, XII-195 pp., 1945.

214. DZIOB, REV. MICHAEL WALTER, J.C.D., The Sacred Congregation for the Oriental Church, XII-181 pp., 1945.

215. EIDENSCHINK, REV. JOHN ALBERT, O.S.B., B.A., J.C.D., The Election of Bishops in the Letters of Pope Gregory the Great, VII-200 pp., 1945. pp., 1945.

216. GILL, REV. NICHOLAS, C.P., J.C.D., The Spiritual Prefect in Clerical Religious Houses of Study, X-140 pp., 1945.

217. HYNES, REV. HARRY GERARD, S.T.L., J.C.D., The Privileges of Cardinals, XII-183 pp., 1945.

218. MCDEVITT, REV. GERARD VINCENT, S.T.L., J.C.D,. The Renunciation of an Ecclesiastical Office, XIV-179 pp., 1945.

219. MANNING, REV. JOSEPH LEROY, J.C.D., The Free Conferral of Offices, VIII-116 pp., 1945.

220. MEYER, REV. LOUIS G., O.S.B., A.B., S.T.B., J.C.D, Alms-gathering by Religious, XII-163 pp., 1945.

221. O'DONNELL, REV. CLETUS FRANCIS, M.A., J.C.D., The Marriage of Minors, XII-268 pp., 1945.

222. PRUNSKIS, REV. JOSEPH, J.C.D., Comparative Law, Ecclesiastical and Civil, in Lithuanian Concordat, X-161 pp., 1945.

223. SWEENEY, REV. FRANCIS PATRICK, C.SS R., J.C.D., The Reduction of Clerics to the Lay State, X-199 pp., 1945.

224 VOGELPOHL, REV. HENRY JOHN, J.C.D., The Simple Impediments to Holy Orders, XVI-190 pp., 1945.

225. BROCKHAUS, REV. THOMAS AQUINAS, O.S.B., J.C.D., Religious Who Are Known as *Conversi*, X-127 pp., 1945.

226. GRIESE, REV. N. ORVILLE, S.T.D., J.C.D., The Marriage Contract and the Procreation of Offspring, XVI-224 pp., 1946.

227. BOUDREAUX, REV. WARREN LOUIS, J.C.D., The *"ab acatholicis nati"* of Canon 1099, § 2, XII-110 pp., 1946.

228. BOWE, REV. THOMAS JOSEPH, A.B., J.C.D., Religious Superioresses,

229. DIEDERICHS, REV. MICHAEL FERDINAND, S.C.J., J.C.D., The Jurisdiction of the Latin Ordinaries Over Their Oriental Subjects, XIV-153 pp., 1946.

230. DINGMAN, REV. MAURICE JOHN, A.B., S.T.L., J.C.L., The Plaintiff in Contentious Trials.

231. FRISON, REV. BASIL, C.M.F., M.MUS., J.C.D., The Retroactivity of Law, X-221 pp., 1946.

232. GALVIN, REV. WILLIAM ANTHONY, M.A., J.C.D., The Administrative Transfer of Pastors, XII-288 pp., 1946.

233. GORACY, REV. JOSEPH C., J.C.L., The Diriment Matrimonial Impediment of Major Orders.

234. HALE, REV. JOSEPH FRANCIS, M.A., S.T.L., J.C.L., The Pastor of Burial.

235. HENRY, REV. JOSEPH ARTHUR, A.B., J.C.D., The Mass and Holy Communion: Inter-Ritual Law, XII-138 pp., 1946.

236. LINENBERGER, REV. HERBERT, C.PP.S., J.C.L., The False Denunciation of an Innocent Confessor.

237. LOWRY, REV. JAMES MARTIN, A.B., J.C.D., Dispensation from Private Vows, XII-266 pp., 1946.

238. LYNCH, REV. GEORGE EDWARD, A.B., S.T.L., J.C.D., Coadjutors and Auxilliaries of Bishops, X-107 pp., 1947.

239. LYNCH, REV. TIMOTHY, M.S.SS.T., J.C.D., Contracts Between Bishops and Religious Congregations, XIV-232 pp., 1946.

240. MCCLUNN, REV. JUSTIN DAVID, A.B., S.T.L., J.C.D., Administrative Recourse, VII-142 pp., 1946.

241. LOHMULLER, REV. MARTIN NICHOLAS, A.B., J.C.D., The Promulgation of Law, XII-140 pp., 1947.

242. MCGRATH, REV. JAMES, A.B., J.C.D., The Privilege of the Canon, XII-156 pp., 1946.

243. MARBACH, REV. JOSEPH FRANCIS, A.B., J.C.D., Marriage Legislation for the Catholics of the Oriental Rites in the United States and Canada, XIV-314 pp., 1946.

244. SHIMKUS, REV. BERNARD ALOYSIUS, A.B., J.C.L., The Determination and Transfer of Rite.

245. SMITH, REV. VINCENT MICHAEL, A.B., S.T.L., J.C.L., Ignorance Affecting Matrimonial Consent.

246. WACHTRLE, REV. PAUL ANTHONY, A.B., J.C.L., The Baptism of the Children of Non-Catholics.

247. CROTTY, REV. MATTHEW MICHAEL, J.C.D., The Recipient of First Holy Communion, X-142 pp., 1947.

248. EAGLETON, REV. GEORGE, J.C.L., The Quinquennial Faculties, Formula IV.

249. GIBBONS, REV. MARION LEO, C.M., LL.B., J.C.D., Domicile of the Wife Unlawfully Separated from Her Husband, XIV-171 pp., 1947.

250. KELLY, REV. BERNARD MATTHEW, S.T.L., J.C.D., The Functions Reserved to Pastors, XII-141 pp., 1947.

251. KILCULLEN, REV. THOMAS JOHN, LL.M., J.C.D., The Collegiate Moral Person as Party Litigant, X-150 pp., 1947.

252. LAFONTAINE, REV. GERMAIN JOSEPH, W.F., J.C.L., Relations Canoniques entre le Missionaire et Ses Superieurs.

253. LANE, REV. LORAS THOMAS, A.B., S.T.L., J.C.L., Matrimonial Procedure in the Ordinary Court of Second Instance.

254. LOVER, REV. JAMES FRANCIS, C.SS.R., J.C.D., The Master of Novices, X-168 pp., 1947.

255. MCNICHOLAS, REV. TIMOTHY JOSEPH, J.C.L., *The Septimæ Manus* Witness.

256. MAROSITZ, REV. JOSEPH JOHN, M.S.C., J.C.D., Obligations and Privileges of Religious Promoted to the Episcopal or Cardinalatial Dignities, XII-180 pp., 1947.

257. MURPHY, REV. FRANCIS JOSEPH, A.B., J.C.D., Legislative Powers of the Provincial Council, XII-158 pp., 1947.

258. O'BRIEN, REV. ROMAEUS WILLIAM, O.CARM., J.C.D., The Provincial Superior in Religious Orders of Men, X-294 pp., 1947.

259. PFALLER, REV. BENEDICT AUGUSTINE, O.S.B., J.C.L., The *Ipso Facto* Effected Dismissal of Religious.

260. POPEK, REV. ALPHONSE SYLVESTER, M.A., J.C.D., The Rights and Obligations of Metropolitans, XVIII-460 pp., 1947.

261. RISTUCCIA, REV. BERNARD JOSEPH, C.M., J.C.L., Quasi-Religious.

262. SONNTAG, REV. NATHANIEL LOUIS, O.F.M.CAP., J.C.D., Censorship of Special Classes of Books, XII-147 pp., 1947.

263. STADLER, REV. JOSEPH NICHOLAS, J.C.L., Frequent Holy Communion.

264. SZAL, REV. IGNATIUS JOSEPH, J.C.L., The Communication of Catholics with Schismatics.

265. WAGNER, REV. URBAN STANLEY, O.F.M.CONV., J.C.D., Parochial Substitute Vicars and Supplying Priests, X-126 pp., 1947.

266. QUINN, REV. JOSEPH, M.A., J.C.L., Documents Required for the Reception of Orders.

267. BENNINGTON, REV. JAMES CLEMENT, A.B., J.C.L., The Recipient of Confirmation.

268. BLAHER, REV. DAMIAN JOSEPH, O.F.M., A.B., J.C.L., The Ordinary Processes in Causes of Beatification and Canonization.

269. CLUNE, REV. ROBERT BELL, B.A., J.C.L., The Judicial Interrogation of the Parties.

270. COURTEMANCHE, REV. BASIL F., B.A., J.C.L., The Total Simulation of Matrimonial Consent.

271. DLOUHY, REV. MAUR JOHN, O.S.B., A.B., J.C.L., The Ordination of Exempt Religious.

272. DONOVAN, REV. JOHN THOMAS, Ph.B., S.T.L., J.C.L., The Clerical Obligations of Canons 138 and 140.

273. FREKING, REV. FREDERICK W., A.B., S.T.B., J.C.L., The Canonical Installation of Pastors.

274. FULTON, REV. THOMAS B., J.C.L. Prenuptial Investigation.

275. GODLEY, REV. JAMES P., J.C.L., The Time and the Place for the Celebration of Mass.

276. KANE, REV. THOMAS A., A.B., B.S., J.C.L., Jurisdiction of Patriarchs until 1439.

277. KENNEDY, REV. ANDREW A., J.C.L., The Annual Pastoral Report to the Local Ordinary.

278. KONRAD, REV. JOSEPH GEORGE, J.C.L., Transfer of Religious.

279. KRESS, REV. ALPHONSE, J.C.L., Contumacy in Ecclesiastical Trials.

280. McCartney, Rev. Marcellus Anthony, O.F.M., M.A., J.C.L., Faculties of Regular Confessors.

281. McCaslin, Rev. Edward Patrick, M.A., S.T.L., J.C.L., The Division of Parishes.

282. McElroy, Rev. Francis J., A.B., J.C.L., The Privileges of Bishops.

283. Quinn, Rev. Stephen, M.S.SS.T., J.C.L., The Relation between the Local Ordinary and Religious of Diocesan Approval.

284. Schneider, Rev. Edelhard Louis, S.D.S., M.A., J.C.L., The Status of Secularized Ex-Religious Clerics.

285. Thompson, Rev. Chester J., A.B.., J.C.L., The Simple Removal from Office.

www.ingramcontent.com/pod-product-compliance
Lightning Source LLC
LaVergne TN
LVHW050228080826
844660LV00012B/495

* 9 7 8 0 8 1 3 2 2 4 5 6 5 *